INTERNATIONAL CENTRE FOR MECHANICAL SCIENCES

COURSES AND LECTURES No. 190

GEORGE LEITMANN

UNIVERSITY OF CALIFORNIA, BERKELEY

COOPERATIVE AND NON-COOPERATIVE MANY PLAYERS DIFFERENTIAL GAMES

COURSE HELD AT THE DEPARTMENT
OF AUTOMATION AND INFORMATION
JULY 1973

UDINE 1974

SPRINGER-VERLAG WIEN GMBH

Originally published by Springer-Verlag Wien New York in 1972

ISBN 978-3-211-81275-4 ISBN 978-3-7091-2914-2 (eBook)
DOI 10.1007/978-3-7091-2914-2

PREFACE

This monograph contains a discussion of some aspects of cooperative and non-cooperative many person differential games, that is, of dynamical systems under the control of a number of agents who cooperate or compete, respectively. The treatment is restricted in several ways. Only two moods of play are considered, Pareto-optimality for cooperation and Nash equilibrium for non-cooperation ; hence, only games with numerical payoffs are included. Furthermore, only necessary conditions and sufficient conditions for "optimal" play are derived ; no existence theorems are provided. Thus, the results presented here are at best but a brick in the edifice of modern game theory whose cornerstone is surely the contribution of von Neumann and Morgenstern.

I am grateful to the Office of Naval Research and to the National Science Foundation for supporting the research on which much of the discussion is based. I also wish to thank Professor William Schmitendorf and Dr. Wolfram Stadler for their critical reading of the manuscript, and Professors Luigi Sobrero and Angelo Marzollo for inviting me to the CISM and thereby providing the impetus for the writing of this monograph.

Berkeley, August 1973 *George Leitmann*

NOTATION

Standard notation is used throughout this book. All vectors, except for the gradient of a scalar-valued function of a vector, or unless noted otherwise, are column vectors. The superscript T denotes transpose of a matrix.

1. INTRODUCTION

1.1. Problem Statement

We shall be concerned with games involving a number of players. The rules of the game assign to each player a cost function of all the players' decisions as well as the sets from which these decisions may be selected.

Suppose there are N players. The rules of the game prescribe mappings

$$J_i(.) : \prod_{i=1}^{N} D_i \to R^1 \qquad i = 1,2,\ldots,N \tag{1.1}$$

where $J_i(.)$ and D_i is the cost function and decision set, respectively, for player i.

Loosely speaking, each player desires to attain the smallest possible cost to himself. If there exists a $d^* \in \prod_{i=1}^{N} D_i$ such that for all $i \in \{1,2,\ldots,N\}$

$$J_i(d^*) \leqslant J_i(d) \quad \forall d \in \prod_{i=1}^{N} D_i \tag{1.2}$$

then d^* is surely a desirable decision N-tuple, for it simultaneously minimizes each player's cost. In general, no such utopia or absolutely cooperative solution exists (see Refs. 1.1 – 1.3) and the players are faced with a dilemma: What mood of play should they adopt ? In other words, how should an optimal decision be defined ?

We shall consider two moods of play, one cooperative and the other competitive. Both of these are due to economists, the former to Pareto (Ref. 1.4) and the latter to Nash (Ref. 1.5), (actually an engineer and a mathematician, respectively).

1.2. Cooperative Play

According to Pareto, a decision N-tuple or joint decision is considered optimal if and only if one of two situations occurs: Adopting another joint decision either results in no change in any of the costs (and hence there is no reason for adopting another decision or it results in a cost increase to at least one player (which is undesirable in view of the cooperative mood of play (*). More precisely, we have the following

---

(*) The philosophy is embodied in "I am willing to forego a gain if it is to be at your expense."

Definition 1.1. A decision N-tuple $d^* \in \prod_{i=1}^{N} D_i$ is Pareto-optimal if and only if for every $d \in \prod_{i=1}^{N} D_i$ either

$$J_i(d) = J_i(d^*) \quad \forall\, i \in \{1,2,\dots,N\}$$

or there is at least one $i \in \{1, 2, \dots, N\}$ such that

$$J_i(d) > J_i(d^*).$$

Starr (Ref. 1.6) has suggested the following example to illustrate Pareto-optimality : Consider a two player game with $D_i \subseteq R^1$, and plot constant cost contours in $D_1 \times D_2$, see Fig. 1.1.

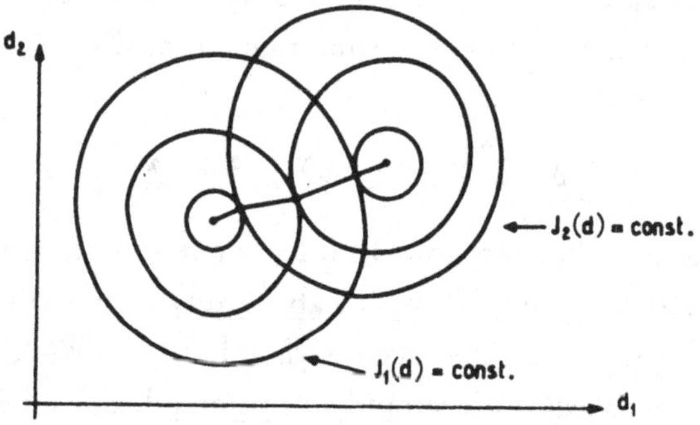

Fig. 1.1 PARETO -- OPTIMALITY
(Arrows indicate direction of decreasing cost)

Then it is readily seen that the points of tangency between equal cost contours of players 1 and 2, respectively, constitute the locus of Pareto-optimal decision couples .

One can readily establish two lemmas which embody sufficiency conditions for Pareto-optimality.

Lemma 1.1. Decision N-tuple $d^* \in \prod_{i=1}^{N} D_i$ is Pareto-optimal if there exists an $\alpha \in R^N$ with $\alpha_i > 0$, $i = 1, 2, \dots, N$, and $\sum_{i=1}^{N} \alpha_i = 1$, such that

$$(1.3) \qquad J(d^*) \leqslant J(d) \quad \forall d \in \prod_{i=1}^{N} D_i$$

where $J(d) = \sum_{i=1}^{N} \alpha_i J_i(d)$.

Proof. Let $d \in \prod_{i=1}^{N} D_i$. Then (1.3) implies either $J(d^*) = J(d)$ or $J(d^*) < J(d)$.

Suppose $J(d^*) = J(d)$. Then, either $J_i(d^*) = J_i(d)$ for all $i \in \{1, 2, ..., N\}$ or there exist $i, j \in \{1, 2, ..., N\}$ such that $J_i(d^*) < J_i(d)$ and $J_j(d^*) > J_j(d)$. If $J(d^*) < J(d)$, then there exists $i \in \{1, 2, ..., N\}$ such that $J_i(d^*) < J_i(d)$.

Thus, the conditions of Pareto-optimality, as given in Definition 1.1, are met.

A slight variation of Lemma 1.1 is

Lemma 1.2. Decision N-tuple $d^* \in \prod_{i=1}^{N} D_i$ is Pareto-optimal if there exists an $\alpha \in R^N$ with $\alpha_i \geq 0, i = 1, 2, ..., N$, and $\sum_{i=1}^{N} \alpha_i = 1$, such that

$$J(d^*) < J(d) \qquad \forall d \in \prod_{i=1}^{N} D_i \,, \; d \neq d^* \tag{1.4}$$

where $J(d) = \sum_{i=1}^{N} \alpha_i J_i(d)$.

Proof. Let $d \in \prod_{i=1}^{N} D_i$. Then (1.4) implies that there exists $i \in \{1, 2, ..., N\}$ such that $J_i(d^*) < J_i(d)$, so that the second condition of Definition 1.1 is met.

Note that these lemmas differ in that the components of α must be strictly positive but the minimum of $J(d)$ need not be unique in Lemma 1.1, whereas in Lemma 1.2 some components of α may be zero but the minimum of $J(d)$ must be unique. Note that a decision N-tuple that yields the unique minimum of any one player's cost is Pareto-optimal; it corresponds to the satisfaction of Lemma 1.2.

For the relation between Pareto-optimal and other moods of cooperative play see Ref. 1.3.

1.3. Non-Cooperative Play

If the players do not cooperate in some sense, that is if they are in strict competition with each player striving to attain the minimum of his own cost regardless of the consequences to the other players, then each player is faced with a problem: In selecting his "best" decision, what should he assume about his opponents' decisions, for they also affect his cost?

Here we shall treat the situation in which each player assumes that his opponents are "rational" and hence choose their decisions so as to minimize their own costs; that is, each player plays with a view towards minimizing his own cost and not towards "hurting" the other players. Thus we are led to the notion of the Nash equilibrium.

Definition 1.2. A decision N-tuple $d^* \in \prod_{i=1}^{N} D_i$ is an equilibrium if and only if for all $i \in \{1,2,\ldots,N\}$

$$J_i(d^*) \leq J_i(d_1^*,\ldots,d_{i-1}^*, d_i, d_{i+1}^*,\ldots, d_N^*)$$

for all $d_i \in D_i$.

To illustrate this notion we turn again to the example suggested by Starr (Ref. 1.6), namely a two player game with $D_i \subseteq R^1$; see Fig. 1.2.

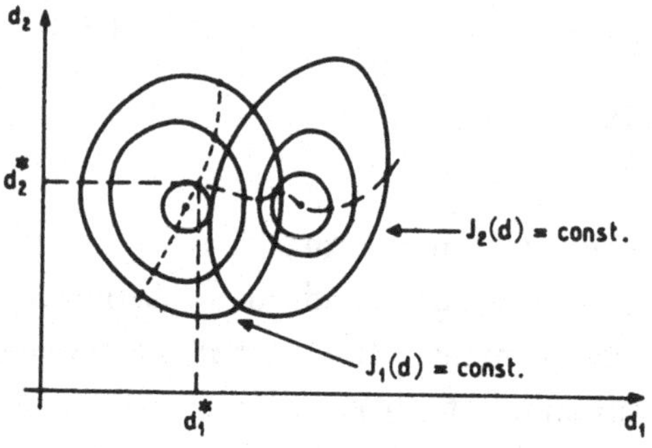

Fig. 1.2 NASH EQUILIBRIUM
(arrows indicate direction of decreasing cost)

For each $d_1 \in D_1$ we determine the $d_2 \in D_2$ that corresponds to the smallest value of $J_2(d)$ and conversely, for each $d_2 \in D_2$ we determine the $d_1 \in D_1$ that yields the smallest value of $J_1(d)$. The loci of these points are shown in Fig. 1.2 ; their intersection in an equilibrium.

An important class of Nash equilibrium games is that of two-person zero-sum games. These are games in which the cost of one player is the negative of the other player's ; that is, one player loses what the other player gains. Thus, we have

(1.5) $$J_1(d) = -J_2(d) = J(d)$$

Hence, in terms of $J(d)$, player 1 is the minimizing player and player 2 is the maximizing one. For such a game we have

Definition 1.3. Decision couple $d^* \in D_1 \times D_2$ is a saddle-point if and only if

$$J(d_1^*, d_2) \leq J(d_1^*, d_2^*) \leq J(d_1, d_2^*)$$

for all $d_1 \in D_1$, $d_2 \in D_2$.

It is readily seen that a saddle-point is an equilibrium; that is, Definition 1.3 is merely one way of stating Definition 1.2 for two-person zero-sum games. Such games have special properties not generally enjoyed by N-person non zero-sum games. Among these are the following:

Lemma 1.3. If both $(d_1^*, d_2^*) \in D_1 \times D_2$ and $(\hat{d}_1, \hat{d}_2) \in D_1 \times D_2$ are saddle-points, then

$$J(d_1^*, d_2^*) = J(\hat{d}_1, \hat{d}_2)$$

Thus, the saddle-point value of $J(d)$ is independent of the saddle-point decision couple; it is called the Value of the game and we shall denote it by J^*.

Lemma 1.4. If both $(d_1^*, d_2^*) \in D_1 \times D_2$ and $(\hat{d}_1, \hat{d}_2) \in D_1 \times D_2$ are saddle-points, then $(d_1^*, \hat{d}_2)$ and $(\hat{d}_1, d_2^*)$ are also saddle-points.

Thus, if the saddle-points are not unique, a decision couple composed of component decisions from different saddle-points is still a saddle-point.

The proofs of Lemmas 1.3 and 1.4 follow directly from Definition 1.3.

Another important property is the following:

Let (d_1^*, d_2^*) be a saddle-point. The use of d_i^* by player i assures him a cost that is at least as favorable as the "best" (smallest or largest, respectively) one he can guarantee to himself. This is embodied in

Lemma 1.5. Let $(d_1^*, d_2^*) \in D_1 \times D_2$ be a saddle-point. Then

$$J(d_1^*, d_2) \leq \underset{d_1 \in D_1}{\text{Min}} \; \underset{d_2 \in D_2}{\text{Sup}} \; J(d_1, d_2) \quad \forall d_2 \in D_2$$

$$J(d_1, d_2^*) \geq \underset{d_2 \in D_2}{\text{Max}} \; \underset{d_1 \in D_1}{\text{Inf}} \; J(d_1, d_2) \quad \forall d_1 \in D_1$$

Proof. Let

$$J(.) : D_1 \times D_2 \rightarrow R^1$$

be the cost function for the two-person zero-sum game. Consider the function

$$\underline{J}(.) : D_2 \to R^1$$

such that for all $d_2 \in D_2$

(1.6) $$\underline{J}(d_2) = \operatorname*{Inf}_{d_1 \in D_1} J(d_1, d_2)$$

Let

(1.7) $$\hat{J} = \operatorname*{Sup}_{d_2 \in D_2} \underline{J}(d_2) = \operatorname*{Sup}_{d_2 \in D_2} \operatorname*{Inf}_{d_1 \in D_1} J(d_1, d_2)$$

Thus,

(1.8) $$\hat{J} \geqslant \underline{J}(d_2) \quad \forall d_2 \in D_2$$

Consider also the function

$$\bar{J}(.) : D_1 \to R^1$$

such that for all $d_1 \in D_1$

(1.9) $$\bar{J}(d_1) = \operatorname*{Sup}_{d_2 \in D_2} J(d_1, d_2)$$

Let

(1.10) $$\tilde{J} = \operatorname*{Inf}_{d_1 \in D_1} \bar{J}(d_1) = \operatorname*{Inf}_{d_1 \in D_1} \operatorname*{Sup}_{d_2 \in D_2} J(d_1, d_2)$$

Thus,

(1.11) $$\tilde{J} \leqslant J(d_1) \quad \forall d_1 \in D_1$$

Now suppose $(d_1^*, d_2^*) \in D_1 \times D_2$ is a saddle-point ; that is,

$$J(\overset{*}{d}_1, d_2) \leqslant J(\overset{*}{d}_1, \overset{*}{d}_2) = \overset{*}{J} \leqslant J(d_1, \overset{*}{d}_2) \quad \forall d_1 \in D_1, d_2 \in D_2 \ . \tag{1.12}$$

By (1.12)

$$\overset{*}{J} = \operatorname*{Inf}_{d_1 \in D_1} J(d_1, \overset{*}{d}_2) = \operatorname*{Min}_{d_1 \in D_1} J(d_1, \overset{*}{d}_2) \tag{1.13}$$

and

$$\overset{*}{J} = \operatorname*{Sup}_{d_2 \in D_2} J(\overset{*}{d}_1, d_2) = \operatorname*{Max}_{d_2 \in D_2} J(\overset{*}{d}_1, d_2) \tag{1.14}$$

By (1.8) with (1.13)

$$\hat{J} \geqslant \overset{*}{J} \tag{1.15}$$

and by (1.11) with (1.14)

$$\tilde{J} \leqslant \overset{*}{J} \tag{1.16}$$

Now if there is a $\hat{d}_2 \in D_2$ such that

$$\hat{J} = \underline{J}(\hat{d}_2) = \operatorname*{Max}_{d_2 \in D_2} \underline{J}(d_2) \tag{1.17}$$

then, by (1.6) with (1.17)

$$\hat{J} = \underline{J}(\hat{d}_2) = \operatorname*{Inf}_{d_1 \in D_1} J(d_1, \hat{d}_2) \leqslant J(d_1, \hat{d}_2) \quad \forall d_1 \in D_1 \ . \tag{1.18}$$

Similarly, if there is a $\tilde{d}_1 \in D_1$ such that

$$\tilde{J} = \bar{J}(\tilde{d}_1) = \min_{d_1 \in D_1} \bar{J}(d_1) \tag{1.19}$$

then, by (1.9) with (1.19),

$$\tilde{J} = \bar{J}(\tilde{d}_1) = \sup_{d_2 \in D_2} J(\tilde{d}_1, d_2) \geqslant J(\tilde{d}_1, d_2) \quad \forall d_2 \in D_2 \tag{1.20}$$

By (1.18) and (1.20)

$$\hat{J} \leqslant J(\tilde{d}_1, \hat{d}_2)$$

and

$$\tilde{J} \geqslant J(\tilde{d}_1, \hat{d}_2)$$

so that

$$\hat{J} \leqslant \tilde{J} \tag{1.21}$$

Then, by (1.15) and (1.16) with (1.21),

$$\hat{J} = \tilde{J} = J^* \tag{1.22}$$

But, by (1.22) with (1.12),

$$J(d_1^*, d_2) \leqslant \hat{J} = \tilde{J} = J^* \leqslant J(d_1, d_2^*) \forall d_1 \in D_1 \quad , \quad d_2 \in D_2 \quad .$$

That is,

$$J(d_1^*, d_2) \leqslant \min_{d_1 \in D_1} \sup_{d_2 \in D_2} J(d_1, d_2) \qquad \forall d_2 \in D_2$$

$$J(d_1, \overset{*}{d_2}) \geqslant \underset{d_2 \in D_2}{\text{Max}} \; \underset{d_1 \in D_1}{\text{Inf}} \; J(d_1, d_2) \qquad \forall d_1 \in D_1$$

which is what we set out to prove. It remains to be shown that the hypotheses leading to (1.17) and (1.19) are met.

By (1.6)

$$\underline{J}(\overset{*}{d_2}) = \underset{d_1 \in D_1}{\text{Inf}} \; J(d_1, \overset{*}{d_2})$$

By (1.12)

$$\underset{d_1 \in D_1}{\text{Inf}} \; J(d_1, \overset{*}{d_2}) = J(\overset{*}{d_1}, \overset{*}{d_2})$$

and

$$J(\overset{*}{d_1}, \overset{*}{d_2}) \geqslant J(\overset{*}{d_1}, d_2) \qquad \forall d_2 \in D_2$$

However, by (1.6),

$$J(\overset{*}{d_1}, d_2) \geqslant \underline{J}(d_2) \qquad \forall d_2 \in D_2$$

Thus,

$$\underline{J}(\overset{*}{d_2}) \geqslant \underline{J}(d_2) \qquad \forall d_2 \in D_2$$

This establishes the validity of the hypothesis leading to (1.17).

Similarly, using (1.9) with (1.12), we show that

$$\bar{J}(\overset{*}{d_1}) \leqslant \bar{J}(d_1) \qquad \forall d_1 \in D_1$$

validating the hypothesis leading to (1.19). This concludes the proof.

In the subsequent chapters we shall apply the concepts discussed in Chapter 1 to a particular class of games, namely <u>differential games</u>. However before doing so it must be stressed that we are restricting the discussion to two moods of play : Pareto-optimality for cooperative games and Nash equilibria for non-cooperative games. Other moods of play are known ; for example, see Refs. 1.3 and 1.7.

References for Chapter 1.

[1.1] Vincent, T.L. and Leitmann, G., Control Space Properties of Cooperative Games, J. Optim. Theory Appl., Vol.6, No. 2, 1970.

[1.2] Leitmann, G., Rocklin, S. and Vincent, T.L., A Note on Control Space Properties of Cooperative Games, J. Optim. Theory Appl., Vol. 9, No. 6, 1972.

[1.3] Yu, P.L. and Leitmann, G., Compromise Solutions, Domination Structures and Salukvadze's Solution, J. Optim. Theory Appl., Vol. 13, No. 3, 1974.

[1.4] Pareto, V., Manuel d'économique politique, Girard et Briere, Paris, 1909.

[1.5] Nash, J., Non-Cooperative Games, Annals of Mathematics, Vol. 54, No. 2, 1951.

[1.6] Ho, Y.C., Differential Games, Dynamic Optimization and Generalized Control Theory, J. Optim. Theory Appl., Vol. 6, No. 3, 1970.

[1.7] Simaan, M. and Cruz, J.B., jr., On the Stackelberg Strategy in Nonzero-Sum Games, J. Optim. Theory Appl., Vol. 11, No. 5, 1973.

2. DYNAMICAL SYSTEMS

2.1. State Equations

We shall be concerned with a dynamical system that is a subset of the universe defined by its state, a set of n real numbers, $x \in R^n$, which change in a prescribed manner with the passing of time $t \in (-\infty, \infty)$(*). The evolution of the state is influenced, or as we say controlled, by N agents whom we shall call players. In particular, we shall deal with a dynamical system whose behavior is governed by ordinary differential equations, the state equations.

Given an initial state x^o at time t_o, we shall be interested in the motion of the state under the control of the players. It is convenient to let time t be one of the state components, say $x_n \equiv t$, and to introduce relative time, $\tau = t - t_o$, henceforth simply called time.

Consider functions

$$u^k(.) : [0,\tau_1] \rightarrow R^{d_k}, \qquad k = 1,2,\ldots,N$$

and C^1 function

$$f(.) : R^n x\ R^{d_1} x\ R^{d_2} x \ldots x\ R^{d_N} \rightarrow R^n$$

The state equation is

$$\dot{x}(\tau) = f(x(\tau), u^1(\tau), u^2(\tau), \ldots, u^N(\tau)) (**) \qquad (2.1)$$

where dot denotes differentiation with respect to τ. For given functions $u^k(.)$ and given initial state x^o, a solution of (2,1) is an absolutely continuous function

$$x(.) : [0,\tau_1] \rightarrow R^n, \quad x(0) = x^o .$$

(*) Of course, any "time like" variable can serve as independent variable.

(**) Of course, $f_n(x(\tau), u^1(\tau), u^2(\tau), \ldots, u^N(\tau)) \equiv 1$

2.2. Controls and Strategies

The players influence the evolutions of the state through their choices of the values $u^k(\tau)$ for almost all $\tau \in [0, \tau_1]$; that is, at time τ player k selects $u^k(\tau)$. Here we shall consider two ways of making these choices : The players utilize either time τ or state $x(\tau)$ as the information on which to base their choices. In the former case, each player selects a function of time on a bounded interval ;player k chooses

$$u^k(.) : [0,\tau_1] \rightarrow R^{d_k}$$

his open-loop control, henceforth simply called control. In the latter case, each player selects a function of the state; player k chooses

$$p^k(.) : R^n \rightarrow R^{d_k}$$

his closed-loop or feedback strategy, henceforth simply called strategy. Then

$$u^k(\tau) = p^k(x(\tau)) \tag{2.2}$$

We shall place certain restrictions on the sets of admissible controls and strategies. These restrictions arise in part from the problem statement and in part from requirements inherent in the subsequent mathematical development. The former restrictions are in the form of constraints on the values of the controls and strategies, respectively.

For $k \in 1,2,...,N$ let $U^k(.) : R^n \rightarrow$ set of all nonempty subsets of R^{d_k} (2.3)

be prescribed set-valued functions. Then, given $x \in R^n$, set $U^k(x)$ is the set of all control or strategy values available to player k at state x.

Definition 2.1. Set K is a set of admissible control N-tuples $u(.) = \{u^1(.), u^2(.), \ldots, u^N(.)\}$ if and only if for all $u(.) \in K$

(i) $u^k(.)$, $k = 1,2,...,N$ is Lebesgue measurable and bounded on interval $[0,\tau_1]$, and

(ii) $u^k(\tau) \in U^k(x)$ for all $x \in R^n$.

Now, given a strategy N-tuple $p(.) = \{p^1(.), p^2(.), \ldots, p^N(.)\}$, let $K^k(x^o)$ denote the set of the $u^k(.)$ corresponding to all solutions $x(.)$, with $x(0) = x^o$, generated by $p(.)$; recall that $u^k(\tau) = p^k(x(\tau))$.

That is, we are allowing here for the possibility of a given strategy N-tuple resulting in non-unique solutions of the state equation for given initial state.

Definition 2.2. Set P is a set of admissible strategy N-tuples p(.) if and only if for all $p(.) \in P$

(i) $$u^k(.) \in K^k(x^\circ), \qquad k = 1,2,\dots,N,$$

is Lebesgue measurable and bounded for all $x^\circ \in R^n$,

(ii) $$p^k(x) \in U^k(x) \quad \text{for all} \quad x \in R^n \,,$$

and

(iii)(*) $\bar{p}(.), \bar{\bar{p}}(.) \in P$, $\bar{x}_n \in (-\infty, \infty)$ and $p(.)$ such that

$$p(x) = \bar{p}(x) \quad \text{for} \quad x_n \leqslant \bar{x}_n$$

$$p(x) = \bar{\bar{p}}(x) \quad \text{for} \quad x_n > \bar{x}_n$$

implies that

$$p(.) \in P$$

2.3. Playability.

Among other motivations, we shall suppose that all players desire to steer the state from a given initial state x° to a state belonging to a prescribed <u>target</u> set, $\theta \subset R^n$.

(*) This technical restriction states that admissible strategy N-tuples can be "joined" along the time axis.

Definition 2.3. A control N-tuple $u(.): [0, \tau_1] \to R^{d_1} \times R^{d_2} \times \ldots \times R^{d_N}$ is playable at x^o if and only if it is admissible and generates a solution(*) $x(.)$ such that $x(0) = x^o$ and $x(\tau_1) \in \theta$. Such a solution is called terminating and τ_1 is the corresponding terminal time. Let $\hat{K}(x^o)$ denote the set of all control N-tuples which are playable at x^o.

Definition 2.4. A strategy N-tuple $p(.) : R^n \to R^{d_1} \times R^{d_2} \times \ldots \times R^{d_N}$ is playable at x^o if and only if it is admissible and generates at least one solution $x(.)$ such that $x(0) = x^o$, $x(\tau) \notin \theta$ for $\tau \in [0, \tau_1)$, and $x(\tau_1) \in \theta$.
Such a solution is called terminating and τ_1 is the corresponding terminal time(**)
A triple $\{x^o, p(.), x(.)\}$, where $x(.)$ is a solution generated by $p(.) \in P$ and $x(0) = x^o$, is termed a play. A play is terminating if and only if $x(.)$ is terminating.

2.4. Performance Index

Associated with each player there is a performance index or cost function.

For a game in which the players utilize controls, given $u(.) \in K$ and $x^o \in R^n$, there is a unique solution of (2.1), $x(.) \in C_a$, where C_a is the class of absolutely continuous functions on bounded intervals. The performance index for player i is

$$V_i(.) : R^n \times K \to R^1 \tag{2.4}$$

For a game in which the players utilize strategies, given $p(.) \in P$ and $x^o \in R^n$, there may be more than one solution of (2.1), $x(.) \in C_a$. The performance index for player i is

$$V_i(.) : R^n \times P \times C_a \to R^1 \tag{2.5}$$

In both cases we shall take the performance index to be such that its value, the cost for player i, is

$$\left.\begin{array}{l} V_i(x^o, u(.)) \\ \\ V_i(x^o, p(.), x(.)) \end{array}\right\} = \int_0^{\tau_1} f_o^i(x(\tau), u^1(\tau), \ldots, u^N(\tau))\,d\tau \tag{2.6}$$

(*) Note that given $u(.) \in K$ and x^o, solution $x(.)$ is unique.

(**) Note that here we require termination the first time the state belongs to θ.

respectively, where the $f^i_o(.)$: $R^n \times R^{d_1} \times \ldots \times R^{d_N} \to R^1$ are of class C^1. Of course, $x(.) : [0, \tau_1] \to R^n$ is a solution of (2.1) generated by u(.) or p(.), respectively, with $x(0) = x^o$.

A more general form of cost is

$$g_i(x(\tau_1)) + \int_0^{\tau_1} f^i_o(x(\tau), u^1(\tau), \ldots, u^N(\tau))d\tau$$

where the $g_i(\cdot) : R^n \to R^1$ are C^1 functions. However, such a cost can always be converted into one of type (2.6), and conversely ; see Appendix A.

While each player desires termination(*), he also wishes to minimize his own cost. He can do so by cooperating with the other players or by competing with them.

Reference for Chapter 2.

[2.1] Isaacs, R., Differential games, Wiley, N.Y., 1965.

[2.2] Blaquière, A., Gérard, F., and Leitmann, G., Quantitative and Qualitative Games, Academic Press, N.Y. 1969.

(*) There are games, such as pursuit evasion games, in which one player desires termination while the other one does not. These are so-called "games of kind" or "qualitative games" ; for instance, see Refs. 2.1 and 2.2.

3. COOPERATIVE DIFFERENTIAL GAMES

3.1. Pareto-optimality

Here we shall consider cooperative play in the sense of Pareto. In particular, we shall restate the definitions and results of Chapter 1 as they apply to the situation discussed in Chapter 2. The definition of Pareto-optimality, Definition 1.1, becomes

Definition 3.1. A control N-tuple $u^*(\cdot) \in \hat{K}(x^\circ)$ is Pareto-optimal if and only if for every $u(.) \in \hat{K}(x^\circ)$ either

$$V_i(x^\circ, u(.)) = V_i(x^\circ, u^*(.)) \quad \forall i \in \{1, 2, \dots, N\}$$

or there is at least one $i \in \{1, 2, \dots, N\}$ such that

$$V_i(x^\circ, u(.)) > V_i(x^\circ, u^*(.)).$$

One question that arises is : Why do the players utilize open-loop controls rather than feedback strategies ? The answer is twofold. First, since the players cooperate by making a joint decision, there appears to be no reason for not announcing their individual decisions. Secondly, as we shall see, the problem eventually reduces to the usual optimal control problem with a single performance index for which, in general, optimal control yields the same result as optimal strategy ; see Ref. 3.1.

It is possible to state conditions that must be fulfilled, necessary conditions, if a control N-tuple is Pareto-optimal ; for instance, see Refs. 3.2 - 3.6. Here we shall proceed differently. We shall give conditions which assure that a control N-tuple is Pareto-optimal, that is sufficient conditions, and then invoke earlier results from optimal control theory to deduce candidates for Pareto-optimality. This appears to be a reasonable approach. For, no matter how we obtain candidates for Pareto-optimality, in the end we are obliged to verify that they are indeed Pareto-optimal ; namely, we must employ sufficient conditions. Then why not proceed from sufficient conditions at the outset ?

And so we recall Lemmas 1.1. and 1.2. For differential games they become

Lemma 3.1. Control N-tuple $u^*(.) \in_N \hat{K}(x^\circ)$ is Pareto-optimal if there exists an $\alpha \in R^N$ with $\alpha_i > 0$, $i = 1, 2, \dots, N$, and $\sum_{i=1} \alpha_i = 1$, such that

$$V(x^\circ,u^*(.)) \leqslant V(x^\circ,u(.)) \quad \forall u(.)\in\hat{K}(x^\circ)$$

where

$$V(x^\circ,u(.)) = \sum_{i=1}^{N} \alpha_i V_i (x^\circ,u(.)).$$

Lemma 3.2. Control N-tuple $u^*(.) \in \hat{K}(x^\circ)$ is Pareto-optimal if there exists an $\alpha \in R^N$ with $\alpha_i \geqslant 0$, $i = 1, 2, \ldots, N$, and $\sum_{i=1}^{N} \alpha_i = 1$, such that

$$V(x^\circ,u^*(.)) < V(x^\circ,u(.)) \quad \forall u(.)\in\hat{K}(x^\circ),\ u(.)\neq u^*(.)(*)$$

where

$$V(x^\circ,u(.)) = \sum_{i=1}^{N} \alpha_i V_i (x^\circ,u(.)).$$

In view of the above lemmas, to deduce control N-tuples which qualify as candidates for Pareto-optimality we need only consider the associated optimal control problem with state equation (2.1), as described in Section 2.1, and with cost $V(x^\circ,u(.))$. That is, to find the control N-tuples which satisfy necessary conditions for Lemmas 3.1 or 3.2, we can invoke results from optimal control theory such as the Maximum Principle; for instance, see Refs. 3.7 - 3.9. In so doing one must bear in mind that such a procedure need not yield all candidates for Pareto-optimality, but only those which are candidates for the sufficient conditions embodied in Lemma 3.1 or 3.2. However, if a control N-tuple satisfies sufficient conditions for the associated optimal control problem, then it meets the conditions of Lemma 3.1 or 3.2, and hence is Pareto-optimal. Based on this observation, we shall now give some sufficient conditions for Pareto-optimality.

3.2. Sufficiency for Pareto-optimality : Prescribed Terminal Time.

In this section we shall present some sufficient conditions for Pareto -optimality in differential games with specified terminal time, τ_1. In principle, this entails no loss of generality since a system with free terminal time can be transformed into one with fixed terminal time ; see Appendix B.

Consider the following associated optimal control problem. The state equation is

$$\dot{x}(\tau) = f(x(\tau), u(\tau)) \tag{3.1}$$

(*) That is $u(\tau) \neq u^*(\tau)$ on a subset of $[0, \tau_1]$ having positive measure.

with $\tau \in [0, \tau_1]$, a specified interval, and

$$(3.2) \qquad x(0) = x^\circ, \quad x(\tau_1) \in \theta$$

where $\{x^\circ\}$ and θ are given sets in R^n. We seek $u^*(.) \in \hat{K}(x^\circ)$ such that

$$(3.3) \qquad V(x^\circ, u^*(.)) \leq V(x^\circ, u(.)) \quad \forall u(.) \in \hat{K}(x^\circ)$$

By adapting sufficient conditions for the problem above (for instance, see Refs. 3.10 - 3.12) we arrive at the following results.

Theorem 3.1. Control N-tuple $u^*(.) \in \hat{K}(x^\circ)$, with corresponding solution $x^*(.)$, is Pareto-optimal if there exist

(a) an $\alpha \in R^N$ with $\alpha_i > 0$, $i = 1, 2, \ldots, N$, and $\sum_{i=1}^{N} \alpha_i = 1$, and

(b) an absolutely continuous $\lambda(.) : [0, \tau_1] \rightarrow R^n$ such that

$$\text{(i)} \qquad \sum_{i=1}^{N} \alpha_i f_o^i(x^*(\tau), u^*(\tau)) - \lambda^T(\tau) f(x^*(\tau), u^*(\tau))$$
$$- \sum_{i=1}^{N} \alpha_i f_o^i(x, u) + \lambda^T(\tau) f(x, u)$$
$$- \dot{\lambda}^T(\tau)[x^*(\tau) - x] \leq 0$$

for all $x \in R^n$ and $u \in \prod_{i=1}^{N} U^i(x)$, and almost all $\tau \in [0, \tau_1]$, and

$$\text{(ii)} \qquad \lambda^T(\tau_1)[x^*(\tau_1) - x] \leq 0$$

for all $x \in \theta$.

Proof. Let $u(.) \in \hat{K}(x^\circ)$, with corresponding solution $x(.)$. By (i) of the theorem with (3.1)

$$\sum_{i=1}^{N} \alpha_i f_o^i(x^*(\tau), u^*(\tau)) - \sum_{i=1}^{N} \alpha_i f_o^i(x(\tau), u(\tau))$$
$$- \frac{d}{d\tau}\left\{\lambda^T(\tau)[x^*(\tau) - x(\tau)]\right\} \leq 0$$

for almost all $\tau \in [0, \tau_1]$. Upon integration with $x^*(0)=x(0)=x^\circ$, and invoking (ii) of the theorem, we obtain

$$V(x^\circ,u^*(.)) \leqslant V(x^\circ,u(.)) \tag{3.4}$$

where

$$V(x^\circ,u(.)) = \sum_{i=1}^{N} \alpha_i \int_0^{\tau_1} f_o^i(x(\tau),u(\tau))d\tau$$

and $u(.) \in \hat{R}(x^\circ)$ is arbitrary. Thus, in view of (3.4) with (a) of the theorem, the conditions of Lemma 3.1. are met, and so $u^*(.)$ is Pareto-optimal.

Appendix A deals with the conversion of a problem with integral cost into an equivalent problem with terminal cost. Let us suppose that this conversion has been accomplished and that we are concerned with costs

$$V_i(x^\circ,u(.)) = g_i(x(\tau_1)) \qquad i = 1,2,\ldots,N$$

Futhermore, let us restrict the target set, θ, to be a smooth manifold in R^n; that is, θ is the intersection of $p \leqslant n$ smooth surfaces whose equations are

$$\theta_i(x) = 0 \qquad i = 1,2,\ldots,p$$

where

$$\theta_i(.) : R^n \to R^1$$

is of class C^1, and the matrix

$$\frac{\partial\theta(x)}{\partial x} = \left[\frac{\partial\theta_i(x)}{\partial x_j}\right] \qquad \begin{matrix} i = 1,2,\ldots,p \\ j = 1,2,\ldots,n \end{matrix}$$

has maximum rank for all $x \in \theta$.

For the problem as restricted above, we have

Theorem 3.2. Let functions $g_i(.)$, $i = 1, 2, \ldots, N$, be convex. Then $u^*(.) \in \hat{R}(x^\circ)$, with corresponding solution $x^*(.)$, is Pareto-optimal if there exist

(a) an $\alpha \in R^N$ with $\alpha_i > 0$, $i = 1, 2, \ldots, N$, and $\sum_{i=1}^{N} \alpha_i = 1$,

(b) a $\nu \in R^p$, and

(c) an absolutely continuous $\lambda(.) : [0, \tau_1] \to R^n$ with

$$\lambda^T(\tau_1) = \text{grad } g\ (x^*(\tau_1)) + \nu^T \frac{\partial\theta(x^*(\tau_1))}{\partial x}$$

where

$$g(x) = \sum_{i=1}^{N} \alpha_i\, g_i\ (x),$$

such that

$$\text{(i)} \qquad \lambda^T(\tau) f(x,u) - \lambda^T(\tau) f(x^*(\tau), u^*(\tau)) + \dot\lambda^T(\tau)\, [x - x^*(\tau)] \geqslant 0$$

for all $x \in R^n$ and $u \in \prod_{i=1}^{N} U^i(x)$, and almost all $\tau \in [0, \tau_1]$, and

$$\text{(ii)} \qquad \nu^T \frac{\partial\theta(x^*(\tau_1))}{\partial x} [x - x^*(\tau_1)] \leqslant 0$$

for all $x \in \theta$.

Proof. Let $u(.) \in \hat{K}(x^\circ)$, with corresponding solution $x(.)$. According to (i) of the theorem

$$\frac{d}{d\tau}\left\{\lambda^T(\tau)[x(\tau) - x^*(\tau)]\right\} \geqslant 0$$

Upon integration with $x^*(0) = x(0) = x^\circ$, we obtain

$$\lambda^T(\tau_1)[x(\tau_1) - x^*(\tau_1)] \geqslant 0$$

so that, in view of (c) with (ii) of the theorem,

$$\text{(3.5)} \qquad \text{grad } g\ (x^*(\tau_1))[x(\tau_1) - x^*(\tau_1)] \geqslant 0$$

Now let

$$V(x^\circ, u(\cdot)) = g(x(\tau_1)) = \sum_{i=1}^{N} \alpha_i\, g_i\ (x(\tau_1)).$$

In view of (a) of theorem , the convexity of the $g_i(.)$ implies the convexity of $g(.)$. Hence

$$V(x^\circ,u(\cdot)) - V(x^\circ,u^*(\cdot)) = g(x(\tau_1)) - g(x^*(\tau_1))$$

$$\geqslant \text{grad } g(x^*(\tau_1))[x(\tau_1) - x^*(\tau_1)]$$

And so it follows by (3.5) that

$$V(x^\circ,u(\cdot)) - V(x^\circ,u^*(\cdot)) \geqslant 0 \tag{3.6}$$

But (3.6) holds for all $u(.) \in \hat{K}(x^\circ)$. Thus, the conditions of Lemma 3.1. are met, and so $u^*(.)$ is Pareto-optimal.

If the problem is restricted further, additional results can be obtained. They are contained in the following corollary to Theorem 2.

Let

$$\frac{\partial f(x,u)}{\partial x} = \left[\frac{\partial f_i(x,u)}{\partial x_j}\right] \qquad \begin{matrix} i = 1,2,\dots,n \\ j = 1,2,\dots,n \end{matrix}$$

$$\frac{\partial f(x,u)}{\partial u} = \left[\frac{\partial f_i(x,u)}{\partial u_j}\right] \qquad \begin{matrix} i = 1,2,\dots,n \\ j = 1,2,\dots,K \end{matrix}$$

where $K = d_1 + d_2 + \dots + d_N$.

Corollary 3.1. Let functions $g_i(.)$, $i = 1, 2, \dots, N$, $f_i(.)$, $i = 1, 2, \dots, n$, and $\theta_i(.)$, $i = 1, 2, \dots, p$, be convex. Then $u^*(.) \in \hat{K}(x^\circ)$, with corresponding solution $x^*(.)$, is Pareto-optimal if there exist

(a) an $\alpha \in R^N$ with $\alpha_i > 0$, $i = 1, 2, \dots, N$, and $\sum_{i=1}^{N} \alpha_i = 1$,

(b) a $\nu \in R^p$ with $z_i \geqslant 0$, $i = 1, 2, \dots, p$, and

(c) an absolutely continuous $\lambda(.) : [0, \tau_1] \to R^n$ satisfying

$$\dot{\lambda}^T(\tau) = -\lambda^T(\tau) \frac{\partial f(x^*(\tau),u^*(\tau))}{\partial x}$$

with

$$\lambda_i(\tau) \geqslant 0 \quad \text{for all} \quad \tau \in [0,\tau_1], \quad i = 1,2,\dots,n$$

and

$$\lambda^T(\tau_1) = \text{grad } g(x^*(\tau_1)) + \nu^T \frac{\partial\theta(x^*(\tau_1))}{\partial x}$$

where

$$g(x) = \sum_{i=1}^{N} \alpha_i g_i(x),$$

such that

$$\text{(i)} \qquad \lambda^T(\tau) \frac{\partial f(x^*(\tau),u^*(\tau))}{\partial u} [u - u^*(\tau)] \geqslant 0$$

for all $u \in \prod_{i=1}^{N} U^i(x)$ and $x \in R^n$, and almost all $\tau \in [0, \tau_1]$.

Proof: By (c), the convexity of the $f_i(.)$ and (i), we have

$$\lambda^T(\tau)f(x,u) - \lambda^T(\tau)f(x^*(\tau),u^*(\tau)) + \dot{\lambda}^T(\tau)[x - x^*(\tau)]$$

$$= \lambda^T(\tau)f(x,u) - \lambda^T(\tau)f(x^*(\tau),u^*(\tau))$$

$$- \lambda^T(\tau) \frac{\partial f(x^*(\tau),u^*(\tau))}{\partial x} [x - x^*(\tau)]$$

$$\geqslant \lambda^T(\tau) \frac{\partial f(x^*(\tau),u^*(\tau))}{\partial u} [u - u^*(\tau)] \geqslant 0$$

Thus, condition (i) of Theorem 3.2 is met.

By the convexity of the $\theta_i(.)$, for $x \in \theta$,

$$0 = \theta_i(x) - \theta_i(x^*(\tau_1)) \geqslant \text{grad } \theta_i(x^*(\tau_1))[x - x^*(\tau_1)]$$

so that for any $\nu \in R^p$ with $\nu_i \geqslant 0$, $i = 1, 2, \dots, p$,

$$\nu^T \frac{\partial\theta(x^*(\tau_1))}{\partial x} [x - x^*(\tau_1)] \leqslant 0$$

and hence condition (ii) of Theorem 3.2 is met.

Condition (a) of the corollary is that of Theorem 3.2, as is the supposition that the $g_i(.)$ are convex. Consequently, all conditions of Theorem 3.2 are satisfied, and so $u^*(.)$ is Pareto-optimal.

Theorems 3.1 and 3.2, and Corollary 3.1, are based on Lemma 3.1. To allow for zero components of α, we utilize Lemma 3.2. By a proof similar to that of Theorem 3.2, one can deduce

Theorem 3.3. Let functions $g_i(.)$, $i = 1, 2, \ldots, N$, be convex. Then $u^*(.) \in \hat{K}(x^\circ)$, with corresponding solution $x^*(.)$, is Pareto-optimal if there exist

(a) an $\alpha \in R^N$ with $\alpha_i \geq 0$, $i = 1,2,\ldots,N$, and $\sum_{i=1}^{N} \alpha_i = 1$,

(b) a $\nu \in R^p$, and

(c) an absolutely continuous $\lambda(.) : [0,\tau_1] \to R^n$ with

$$\lambda^T(\tau_1) = \text{grad } g(x^*(\tau_1)) + \nu^T \frac{\partial\theta(x^*(\tau_1))}{\partial x}$$

where

$$g(x) = \sum_{i=1}^{N} \alpha_i g_i(x),$$

such that, for all $u(.) \in \hat{K}(x^\circ)$, $u(.) \neq u^*(.)$, with corresponding solution $x(.)$,

(i)
$$\lambda^T(\tau) f(x(\tau), u(\tau)) - \lambda^T(\tau) f(x^*(\tau), u^*(\tau)) + \dot{\lambda}^T(\tau)[x(\tau) - x^*(\tau)] \geq 0$$

for almost all $\tau \in [0,\tau_1]$, with strict inequality holding on a subset of $[0, \tau_1]$ having positive measure, and

(ii)
$$\nu^T \frac{\partial\theta(x^*(\tau_1))}{\partial x} [x(\tau_1) - x^*(\tau_1)] \leq 0.$$

Theorem 3.3. has a corollary that is analogous to Corollary 3.1.

3.3. Sufficiency for Pareto-optimality : Unspecified Terminal Time.

In section 3.2. we considered the associated optimal control problem with prescribed terminal time. Here we shall give a different kind of sufficiency theorem that is applicable whether or not τ_1 is specified. If τ_1 is not fixed, $x_n(0)$ and $x_n(\tau_1)$ are not given, however, if τ_1 is fixed, $x_n(0)$ and $x_n(\tau_1)$ are prescribed. The first theorem is based on one given in Ref. 3.13.

Theorem 3.4. Let X be an open subset of R^n. Control N-tuple $u^*(.) \in \hat{K}(x^\circ)$, with corresponding solution $x^*(.) : [0,\tau_1^*] \to R^n$, is Pareto-optimal with respect to any $u(.) \in \hat{K}(x^\circ)$ with corresponding solution $x(.) : [0,\tau_1] \to R^n$ such that $x(\tau) \in X$ for all $\tau \in [0,\tau_1]$, if there exist

(a) an $\alpha \in R^n$ with $\alpha_i > 0$, $i = 1,2,\dots,N$, and $\sum_{i=1}^{N} \alpha_i = 1$, and

(b) a C^1 function $V(.) : \overline{X} \to R^1$ such that

(i) (*) $V(x) = 0$ for all $x \in \theta \cap \overline{X}$,

(ii) $$\int_0^{\tau_1^*} \left[\sum_{i=1}^{N} \alpha_i f_o^i(x^*(\tau), u^*(\tau)) + \operatorname{grad} V(x^*(\tau)) f(x^*(\tau), u^*(\tau))\right] d\tau = 0,$$

and

(iii) $$\sum_{i=1}^{N} \alpha_i f_o^i(x,u) + \operatorname{grad} V(x) f(x,u) \geq 0$$

for all $x \in X$ and $u \in \prod_{i=1}^{N} U^i(x)$.

Proof. Consider $u(.) \in \hat{K}(x^\circ)$ with corresponding solution $x(.) : [0,\tau_1] \to R^n$ such that $x(\tau) \in X$ for all $\tau \in [0,\tau_1]$.

By (i) and state equation (3.1)

$$I = \int_0^{\tau_1} \operatorname{grad} V(x(\tau)) f(x(\tau), u(\tau)) d\tau = -V(x^\circ)$$

Then by (ii)

$$\int_0^{\tau_1^*} \sum_{i=1}^{N} \alpha_i f_o^i(x^*(\tau), u^*(\tau)) d\tau = V(x^\circ)$$

(*) This can be replaced by the weaker condition that $\lim_{\tau \to \tau_1} V(x(\tau)) = 0$, $x(\tau_1) \in \theta$.

Now consider

$$\Delta = \int_0^{\tau_1} \sum_{i=1}^{N} \alpha_i f_o^i (x(\tau), u(\tau)) d\tau - \int_0^{\tau_1^*} \sum_{i=1}^{N} \alpha_i f_o^i (x^*(\tau), u^*(\tau)) d\tau$$

Now add the null term I + V(x°) to Δ, so that

$$\Delta = \int_0^{\tau_1} \left[\sum_{i=1}^{N} \alpha_i f_o^i (x(\tau), u(\tau)) + \text{grad } V(x(\tau)) f(x(\tau), u(\tau)) \right] d\tau$$

Finally, by (iii), $\Delta \geqslant 0$. This, together with condition (a), meets the requirements of Lemma 3.1. This concludes the proof.

Because of the smoothness required of function V(.), Theorem 3.4 is applicable to a restricted class of problems. Below we state a sufficiency theorem that is applicable to a wider class of problems. The theorem is stated without proof ; the proof may be found in Ref. 3.14. Before giving the theorem we need some definitions.

Definition 3.1. A <u>denumerable decomposition</u> D of a set $X \subseteq R^n$ is a denumerable collection of pairwise disjoint subsets whose union is X. We shall write $D = \{ X_j : j \in J \}$ where J is a denumerable index set of the pairwise disjoint subsets.

Definition 3.2. Let X be a subset of R^n and D a denumerable decomposition of X. A continuous $V(.) : X \to R^1$ is continuously differentiable with respect to D if and only if there exists a collection $\{ (W_j, V_j) : j \in J \}$ such that W_j is an open set containing X_j, $V_j(.) : W_j \to R^1$ is continuously differentiable, and

$V_j(x) = V(x)$ for $x \in X_j$.

Now we are ready to state

Theorem 3.5. Let X be a subset of R^n. Control N-tuple $u^*(.) \in \hat{K}(x^\circ)$, with corresponding solution $x^*(.) : [0, \tau_1^*] \to R^n$, is Pareto-optimal with respect to any $u(.) \in \hat{K}(x^\circ)$, with corresponding solution $x(.) : [0, \tau_1] \to R^n$ such that $x(\tau) \in X$ for all $\tau \in [0, \tau_1)$, if there exist

(a) an $\alpha \in R^n$ with $\alpha_i > 0$, $i = 1,2,\dots,N$, and $\sum_{i=1}^{N} \alpha_i = 1$, and

(b) a denumerable decomposition D of X, a continuous function $V(.) : X \to R^1$ which is continuously differentiable with respect to D, and a collection $\{(W_j, V_j) : j \in J\}$, such that

(i) $V(x) = 0$ for all $x \in \theta \cap X$,

(ii) $$\sum_{i=1}^{N} \alpha_i f_o^i(x^*(\tau), u^*(\tau)) + \text{grad } V_j(x^*(\tau)) f(x^*(\tau), u^*(\tau)) = 0$$

almost everywhere in T_j^* for all $j \in J$, where $T_j^* = \{\tau \in [0, \tau_1^*] : x^*(\tau) \in X_j\}$, and

(iii) $$\sum_{i=1}^{N} \alpha_i f_o^i(x,u) + \text{grad } V_j(x) f(x,u) \geqslant 0$$

for all $x \in X_j$, $u \in \prod_{i=1}^{N} U^i(x)$, and $j \in J$.

Note that Theorems 3.4 and 3.5 are "local" sufficiency theorems since they establish Pareto-optimality in a subset of playable control N-tuples, namely those which generate solutions which belong to a subset of R^n. Finally, note that, in addition to the constrainsts on $u(\tau)$, state constraints of the form $x(\tau) \in B$ for all $\tau \in [0, \tau_1]$, given $B \subset R^n$, can be considered by letting $X = B$ in Theorem 3.5.

3.4. Example : Collective Bargaining(*)

We consider a process of negotiation between management and union during a strike. In this process, the state at time τ is defined by two variables(**) : the offer by management, $x(\tau)$, and the demand by the union, $y(\tau)$. If x° and y° denote initial offer and demand, respectively, then $y^\circ > x^\circ$.

We adopt the following model :

1) The two sides make offer and demand by a process described by

$$\dot{x}(\tau) = u(\tau)[y(\tau) - x(\tau)]$$

(*) Based on Ref. 3.15

(**) As can be readily verified, time, t, enters all conditions trivially ; hence, it need not be considered as a state component.

$$y(\tau) = - v(\tau)[y(\tau) - x(\tau)]$$

$$u(\tau) \in [0,a], \quad v(\tau) \in [0,b]$$

where $u(\tau)$ and $v(\tau)$ are chosen by management and union, respectively, and positive constants a, b are given. That is, the rates of change of offer and demand depend linearly on "how far apart" the negotiators are, with the slopes under the respective control of management and union.

2) Agreement is reached at time τ_1, the smallest value of τ for which

$$y(\tau) - x(\tau) = m$$

where m is a given positive number ; that is, the union agrees to end the strike when the offer is sufficiently close to the demand.

3) Both sides desire on early end of the strike. However, management desires to minimize the terminal offer, $x(\tau_1)$, whereas the union wishes to maximize its terminal demand, $y(\tau_1)$. So we postulate the following costs

$$k_1\tau_1 + x(\tau_1) \quad \text{for management}$$

$$k_2\tau_1 - y(\tau_1) \quad \text{for union}$$

where k_1, k_2 are given, positive constants.

In terms of $z(\tau) = y(\tau) - x(\tau)$, we have

$$\dot{z}(\tau) = - [u(\tau) + v(\tau)]z(\tau) \tag{3.7}$$

with initial condition

$$z(0) = z^\circ = y^\circ - x^\circ$$

and target set

$$\theta = \{z : z - m = 0\} \tag{3.8}$$

The control constraints are

$$0 \leq u(\tau) \leq a \;,\; 0 \leq v(\tau) \leq b \tag{3.9}$$

and the costs are(*)

$$\begin{aligned} V_1(z^\circ, u(.), v(.)) &= \int_0^{\tau_1} [k_1 + u(\tau) z(\tau)] d\tau \\ V_2(z^\circ, u(.), v(.)) &= \int_0^{\tau_1} [k_2 + v(\tau) z(\tau)] d\tau \end{aligned} \tag{3.10}$$

We seek Pareto-optimal control couples { $u^*(.)$, $v^*(.)$ } with corresponding solutions $z^*(.) : [\,0, \tau_1{}^*] \to R^1$. And so we consider the associated optimal control problem with cost

$$V(z^\circ, u(.), v(.)) = \sum_{i=1}^{z} \alpha_i V_i (z^\circ, u(.), v(.)) \tag{3.11}$$

where $\alpha \in R^2$ with $\alpha_i \geq 0$ and $\sum_{i=1}^{N} \alpha_i = 1$; that is we seek to satisfy Lemma 3.2.

Cost (3.11) can be rewritten as

$$V(z^\circ, u(.), v(.)) = \int_0^{\tau_1} [k + \beta\; u(\tau) z(\tau)] d\tau \tag{3.12}$$

where constant terms have again been dropped, and $k = \alpha_1 k_1 + \alpha_2 k_2$, $\beta = \alpha_1 - \alpha_2$.

Upon utilizing the necessary conditions of the Maximum Principle (the details may be found in Ref. 3.14) we obtain a unique candidate for Pareto-optimality for every choice of α. We have three cases :

I. $\alpha_1 > \alpha_2$

1) $\frac{k}{\beta b} \geq m$

$$u^*(\tau) = \begin{cases} 0 & \text{for } z^*(\tau) \geq \frac{k}{\beta b} \\ a & \text{for } z^*(\tau) < \frac{k}{\beta b} \end{cases} \;,\; v^*(\tau) \equiv b$$

(*) Here we have disregarded terms depending only on x^0, y^0.

2) $\frac{k}{\beta b} < m$

$u^*(\tau) \equiv 0 \quad , \quad v^*(\tau) \equiv b$

II. $\alpha_1 = \alpha_2$

$u^*(\tau) \equiv a \quad , \quad v^*(\tau) \equiv b$

III. $\alpha_1 < \alpha_2$

1) $-\frac{k}{\beta a} \geqslant m$

$$u^*(\tau) \equiv a \ , \ v^*(\tau) = \begin{cases} 0 & \text{for} \quad z^*(\tau) \geqslant -\frac{k}{\beta a} \\ b & \text{for} \quad z^*(\tau) < -\frac{k}{\beta a} \end{cases}$$

2) $-\frac{k}{\beta a} < m$

$u^*(\tau) \equiv a \ , \ v^*(\tau) \equiv 0$

To establish the Pareto-optimality of these candidates, we invoke Theorem 3.5. To illustrate its utilization, let us consider case I. Here

$$X = \{z : z \in [m, \infty)\}$$

For subcase 1) we require a decomposition with

$$X_1 = \left\{z : z \in \left[m, \frac{k}{\beta b}\right)\right\}$$

$$X_2 = \left\{z : z \in \left[\frac{k}{\beta b}, \infty\right)\right\}$$

and where

(*) In fact, $V(\cdot)$ is C^1 so that Theorem 3.4 can be used.

$$V_1(z) = \frac{k}{a+b} \ln \frac{z}{m} + \frac{\beta a}{a+b}(z-m)$$

$$V_2(z) = \frac{k}{b} \ln z + c$$

with c chosen to insure continuity at

$$z = \frac{k}{\beta b}.$$

For subcase 2) we do not require a decomposition ; we choose

$$V(z) = \frac{k}{b} \ln \frac{z}{m}$$

Now it is readily seen that the conditions of Theorem 3.5. are met, and so the candidates are indeed Pareto-optimal.

Finally, note that the Pareto-optimal controls are given in feedback form, that is, knowledge of the state, $z^*(\tau)$, determines the values of $u^*(\tau)$ and $v^*(\tau)$; see Appendix C.

3.5. Example : Advertising.

Here we consider a problem based on one suggested by Starr (Ref. 3.16). The divisions of a conglomerate company are in competition and wish to use their advertising revenue in the "best" way, that is to maximize their individual profits. Yet, being divisions of a parent company, they are not out to "hurt" each other ; thus, a cooperative game solution appears reasonable.

Let $x_i(\tau)$ = rate of demand of i-th division's product = gross revenue per day of i-th division

c_i = fraction of revenue left after marginal costs.

$u_i(\tau)$ = rate of expenditure for advertising.

To be specific, we consider two divisions and suppose that changes in the rates of demand are given by

$$\dot{x}_1(\tau) = 12\, u_1(\tau) - 2u_1^2(\tau) - x_1(\tau) - u_2(\tau)$$

$$\dot{x}_2(\tau) = 12\, u_2(\tau) - 2u_2^2(\tau) - x_2(\tau) - u_1(\tau)$$

$$\text{with} \quad x_i(0) = x_i^\circ \quad \text{and}$$

$$u_i(\tau) \geqslant 0$$

The costs (here profits) are

$$V_i(x^\circ, u(.)) = \int_0^{\tau_1} \left[\frac{1}{3} x_i(\tau) - u_i(\tau) \right] d\tau \qquad i = 1,2$$

and these are to be maximized for $\tau \in [0, 1]$.(*)

On applying necessary conditions for the associated optimal control problem, one finds the following candidates for Pareto-optimality :

$$u_i^*(\tau) = \begin{cases} \frac{3}{4}\left(e^{\tau-1} - 1\right)^{-1} + 3 - \frac{\alpha_j}{4\alpha_i} & \text{for } \tau \in [0, \tau_i] \\ 0 & \text{for } \tau \in (\tau_i, 1] \end{cases}$$

if $\frac{\alpha_j}{\alpha_i} < 3\left(e^{-1} - 1\right)^{-1} + 12$, and $u_i^*(\tau) \equiv 0$ for $\tau \in [0,1]$

if $\frac{\alpha_j}{\alpha_i} \geqslant 3\left(e^{-1} - 1\right)^{-1} + 12$, where $\tau_i = 1 + \ln\left[1 + 3\left(\frac{\alpha_j}{\alpha_i} - 12\right)^{-1}\right]$

for $i = 1,2$ $(j = 2,1)$, and $\alpha_1, \alpha_2 > 0$, $\alpha_1 + \alpha_2 = 1$

Using

$$\lambda_i(\tau) = \frac{1}{3} \alpha_i \left(e^{\tau-1} - 1\right) \qquad i = 1,2$$

obtained from the necessary conditions, one can use Theorem 3.1. to establish that the candidates are indeed Pareto-optimal (see Ref. 3.12).

(*) Since the time interval is fixed, we must consider $t = x_3$; that is, $\dot{x}_3(\tau) = 1$, $x_3(0) = 0$, $x_3(\tau_1) = 1$.

References for Chapter 3.

[3.1] Leitmann, G., A Note on Optimal Open-Loop and Closed-Loop Control, J. Dynamical Systems, Measurement, and Control, Vol.98, No. 3, 1974.

[3.2] Da Cunha, N.O. and Polak, E., Constrained Minimization under Vector-Valued Criteria in Linear Topological Spaces, in Mathematical Theory of Control (eds. Balakrishnan, A.V. and Neustadt, L.W.), Academic Press, N. Y. 1967.

[3.3] Vincent, T.L. and Leitmann, G., Control Space Properties of Cooperative Games, J. Optim. Theory Appl., Vol. 6, No. 2, 1970.

[3.4] Leitmann, G., Rocklin, S., and Vincent, T.L., A Note on Control Space Properties of Cooperative Games, J. Optim. Theory Appl., Vol. 9, No. 6, 1972.

[3.5] Stalford, H., Criteria for Pareto-optimality in Cooperative Differential Games, J. Optim. Theory Appl., Vol. 9, No. 6. 1972.

[3.6] Blaquière, A., Juricek, L., and Wiese, K., Geometry of Pareto Equilibria and a Maximum Principle in N-Person Differential Games, J. Math. Anal. Appl. Vol. 38, No., 1, 1972.

[3.7] Pontryagin, L.S., Boltynskii, V.G., Gamkrelidze, R.V., and Mishchenko, E.F., The Mathematical Theory of Optimal Processes, Interscience Publ., N. Y., 1962.

[3.8] Athans, M. and Falb, P.L., Optimal Control,McGraw-Hill, N. Y., 1966.

[3.9] Leitmann, G., An Introduction to Optimal Control, McGraw-Hill, N. Y., 1966.

[3.10] Leitmann, G., and Stalford, H., A Sufficiency Theorem for Optimal Control J. Optim. Theory Appl., Vol. 8, No. 3, 1971.

[3.11] Mangasarian, O.L., Sufficient Conditions for the Optimal Control of Nonlinear Systems, SIAM J. Control, Vol. 4, No. 1, 1966.

[3.12] Leitmann, G., and Schmitendorf, W., Some Sufficiency Conditions for Pareto-optimal Control, J. Dynamical Systems, Measurement and Control, Vol. 95, No. 3, 1963.

[3.13] Leitmann, G., Sufficiency for Optimal Control, J. Optim. Theory Appl., Vol. 2, No. 5, 1968.

[3.14] Stalford, H., Sufficient Conditions for Optimal Control with State and Control Constraints, J. Optm. Theory Appl., Vol. 7, No. 2, 1971.

[3.15] Leitmann, G., and Liu, P.T., A Differential Game Model of Labor-Management Negotiation During a Strike, J. Optim. Theory Appl. Vol. 13, No. 4, 1974.

[3.16] Starr, A.W., Non-zero Sum Differential Games : Concepts and Models, Division of Engineering and Applied Physics Tech.Report 590, Harvard University, Cambridge, 1969.

4. NON–COOPERATIVE DIFFERENTIAL GAMES

4.1. Nash Equilibrium

Here we shall consider non-cooperative play in the sense of Nash. Again, we shall restate the definitions and results of Chapter 1 as they apply to the situation discussed in Chapter 2.

The definition of Nash equilibrium, Definition 1.2, becomes

Definition 4.1. A strategy N-tuple $p^*(.)$ is a Nash equilibrium on a set $X \subseteq R^n$ if and only if

(i) it is playable at all $x^\circ \in X$,

and for all $i \in \{1, 2, \ldots, N\}$ and all $x^\circ \in X$,

(ii) $V_i(x^\circ, p^*(.), x^*(.)) \leq V_i(x^\circ, {}^ip(.), {}^ix(.))$ for all terminating plays $\{x^o, p^*(.), x^*(.)\}$ and $\{x^o, {}^ip(.), {}^ix(.)\}$ where

$${}^ip(.) = \{p^{1*}(.), \ldots, p^{i-1*}(.), p^i(.), p^{i+1*}(.), \ldots, p^{N*}(.)\},$$

and

(iii) $V_i(x^\circ, p^*(.), x^*(.)) = V_i(x^\circ, p^*(.), x^{**}(.))$

for any two terminating plays $\{x^\circ, p^*(.), x^*(.)\}$ and $\{x^\circ, p^*(.), x^{**}(.)\}$.

Some remarks are in order concerning the definition above. First, the reason for the players utilizing feedback strategies is the absence of knowledge about their opponents'decisions : One way a player can gain information about his opponents' decisions: is by observing the state, for its evolution is governed by all the players' decisions. Thus, we shall suppose that the players base their decisions on the current state(*). Secondly, condition (iii) of Definition 4.1. is a technical requirement to assure a Value of the game to each player. We also note by (2.6) that

$$V_i(x^\circ, {}^ip(.), {}^ix(.)) = 0 \qquad \forall x \in \theta$$

and, in particular, that

$$V_i(x^\circ, p^*(.), x^*(.)) = 0 \qquad \forall x \in \theta \tag{4.1}$$

(*) Other schemes are possible; for instance, a player might have to use earlier state information because of delays (see Ref. 4.1 and 4.2).

since, in view of Definition 2.4, termination takes place the first time the state belongs to the target set. Consequently, the conditions of Definition 4.1. are met trivially for $x^\circ \in \theta$; that is, a Nash equilibrium on X is also one on $X^* = X \cup \theta$(*). Thus, for a given equilibrium strategy N-tuple, $p^*(.)$, there are functions

$$V_i^*(.) \; : X^* \to R^1 \qquad i = 1,2,\ldots,N \tag{4.2}$$

such that

$$V_i^*(x^\circ) = V_i(x^\circ, p^*(.), x^*(.)) \tag{4.3}$$

for all terminating plays $\{x^\circ, p^*(.), x^*(.)\}$ and all $x^\circ \in X^*$.

Lastly, we require condition (ii) to be met for all $x^\circ \in X$. That is, $p^*(.)$ is to be an equilibrium no matter at what state play is initiated.

In the following sections we shall derive necessary conditions for a Nash equilibrium for certain classes of such equilibria. For earlier discussions see Refs. 4.3 - 4.6.

4.2. Trajectories, Game and Isovalue Surfaces

In this section we shall introduce some additional concepts and derive some preliminary results.

For each player $i \in \{1,2,\ldots,N\}$ let

$$y^i = (x_0^i, x) \in R^{n+1}$$

denote an augmented state. Given a play

$$\{x^\circ, p(.), x(.)\} \text{ with } x(.):[0,\tau_1] \to R^n,$$

not necessarily terminating, consider the absolutely continuous variable

$$x_0^i(.):[0,\tau_1] \to R^1$$

such that

$$\dot{x}_0^i(\tau) = f_0^i(x(\tau), u(\tau)) \tag{4.4}$$

(*) While it is possible to consider $\theta \not\subset X$, termination requires $\theta \cap \bar{X} \neq \phi$.

with

$$x_o^i(0) = x_o^{io}$$

so that

(4.5) $$x_o^i(\tau_1) - x_o^{io} = \int_o^{\tau_1} f_o^i(x(\tau),u(\tau))d\tau = V_i(x^\circ,p(.),x(.))$$

Next introduce C^1 functions

$$g^i(.) : R^{n+1} \times R^{d_1} \times \ldots \times R^{d_N} \to R^{n+1} \qquad i = 1,2,\ldots,N$$

such that

(4.6)
$$g_o^i(y^i,u) = f_o^i(x,u)$$
$$g_j^i(y^i,u) = f_j(x,u) \qquad j = 1,2,\ldots,n$$

Then, state equation (2,1) can be combined with (4.4) to give the augmented state equation for each player $i \in \{1, 2, \ldots, N\}$

(4.7) $$\dot{y}^i(\tau) = g^i(y^i(\tau),u(\tau))$$

with

$$y^i(0) = y^{io} = (x_o^{io}, x^\circ).$$

The <u>target</u> set in augmented state space is

$$Ⓗ = R^1 \times \theta$$

Hereafter we shall restrict the target set, θ, to be a <u>closed</u> set in R^n with smooth boundary $\partial\theta$; that is

(4.8) $$x \in \partial\theta \Rightarrow x \in \{x : \theta(x) = 0\}$$

where $\theta(.) : R^n \to R^1$ is of class C^1 and grad $\theta(x) \neq 0$ for all x in an open set containing $\partial\theta$. Thus,

$$y^i \in \partial Ⓗ \Rightarrow y^i \in \{y^i ; Ⓗ(y^i) = 0\}$$

where $Ⓗ(.) : R^{n+1} \to R^1$ is of class C^1 such that $Ⓗ(y^i) = \theta(x)$ and grad $Ⓗ(y^i) = (0, \text{grad}\, \theta(x))$.

Definition 4.2. Let $\{x^\circ, p(.), x(.)\}$ be a play with $x(.) : [0,\tau_1] \to R^n$ not necessarily terminating. A <u>trajectory in R^n</u> generated by play $\{x^\circ, p(.), x(.)\}$ is

$$\pi = \{x : x = x(\tau), \tau \in [0,\tau_1]\} \tag{4.9}$$

Here we note that condition (iii) of Definition 2.2 assures that trajectories can be "joined". Namely, consider plays $\{\bar{x}^\circ, \bar{p}(.), \bar{x}(.)\}$ and $\{\bar{\bar{x}}^\circ, \bar{\bar{p}}(.), \bar{\bar{x}}(.)\}$ with $\bar{x}(.) : [0,\bar{\tau}_1]$ and $\bar{\bar{x}}(.):[0,\bar{\bar{\tau}}_1]$ and trajectories $\bar{\pi}$ and $\bar{\bar{\pi}}$, respectively, such that $\bar{x}(\bar{\tau}_1) = \bar{\bar{x}}(0) = \bar{\bar{x}}^\circ$. Then there exists a play $\{\bar{x}^\circ, p(.), x(.)\}$ generating a trajectory $\pi = \bar{\pi} \cup \bar{\bar{\pi}}$.

Definition 4.3. Let $\{x^\circ, {}^ip(.), x^i(.)\}$ be a play with $x^i(.) : [0,\tau_1] \to R^n$, and consider the solution of (4.7), $y^i(.) : [0,\tau_1] \to R^{n+1}$, with

$$x_0^i(\tau) + \int_\tau^{\tau_1} f_0^i(x^i(\xi), {}^ip(x^i(\xi)))d\xi = C \tag{4.10}$$

where C is a given constant. A trajectory in R^{n+1} generated by play $\{x^\circ, {}^ip(.), x^i(.)\}$ is

$$\pi_i(C) = \{y^i : y^i = y^i(\tau), \tau \in [0,\tau_1]\} \tag{4.11}$$

Thus, given a play $\{x^\circ, {}^ip(.), x^i(.)\}$, there is one trajectory in R^n, π, and a one-parameter family of trajectories in R^{n+1}, $\{\pi_i(C)\}$; see Fig. 4.1.

Fig. 4.1 Trajectories

If ${}^ip(.) = p^*(.)$, we denote a corresponding solution of (4.7) by $y^{i*}(.) : [0, \tau_1] \to R^{n+1}$ and trajectory by $\pi_i^*(C)$. If such a solution is terminating, namely

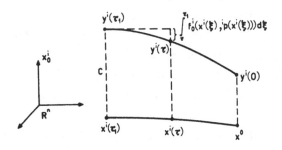

$$y^{i*}(.):[0,\tau_1^*]\to R^{n+1} \text{ with } y^{i*}(\tau_1^*)\in Ⓗ ,$$

we term it and a corresponding trajectory optimal (in the sense of the Nash equilibrium).

Let $P^*(.)$ be an equilibrium on X, generating a terminating solution $x^*(.) : [0,\tau_1^*] \to R^n$. Then the projections on R^n of the members of $\{\pi_i^*(C)\}$ for all $i\in\{1, 2, \ldots, N\}$ are the same optimal trajectory in R^n

$$\pi^* = \{x : x = x^*(\tau), \tau\in[0,\tau_1^*]\}$$

Since function $V_i^*(.)$ is defined on X^* for each player $i \in\{1, 2, \ldots, N\}$ we can state

Definition 4.4. A game surface for player i is

$$\Sigma_i(C) = \{y^i : x_o^i + V_i^*(x) = C, x\in X^*\} \tag{4.12}$$

where C is a constant parameter. The intersection of $\Sigma_i(C)$ with R^n is an isovalue surface

$$S_i(C) = \{y^i : x_o^i = 0, V_i^*(x) = C, x \in X^*\}$$

Note that $S_i(C)$ is the locus of all initial states for which the i-th player's game Value is the same. Again, for each player there is a one-parameter family of game surfaces, $\{\Sigma_i(C)\}$, and a corresponding one-parameter family of isovalue surfaces, $\{S_i(C)\}$.

Given C, (4.12) defines a set of points which are in one-to-one correspondence with the points of X^*. The members of $\{\Sigma_i(C)\}$ are deduced from one another by translation along the x_o^i-axis and are ordered by parameter C. Thus, one and only member of $\{\Sigma_i(C)\}$ passes through a given point of $R^1 \times X^*$.

A given game surface, $\Sigma_i(C)$, separates $R^1 \times X^*$ into two disjoint sets

$$A/\Sigma_i(C) = \{y^i : x_o^i > C - V_i^*(x), x \in X^*\}$$
$$B/\Sigma_i(C) = \{y^i : x_o^i < C - V_i^*(x), x \in X^*\} \tag{4.13}$$

denoting points "above" and "below" $\Sigma_i(C)$, respectively.

A game surface, $\Sigma_i(C)$, that contains a point $y^{io} = (x_o^{io}, x^o)$, according to Definition 4.4, is defined by

$$\Phi_i(y^i) = C = x_o^{io} + V_i^*(x^o)$$

where function

$$\Phi_i(.) : R^1 \times X^* \to R^1$$

is such that

$$\Phi_i(y^i) = x_o^i + V_i^*(x) \qquad (4.14)$$

We are now ready to state a fundamental property of game surfaces.

Theorem 4.1. Consider a strategy N-tuple $p^*(.)$ that is a Nash equilibrium on X and an admissible strategy N-tuple

$$^ip(.) = \{p^{1*}(.), \dots, p^{i-1*}(.), p^i(.), p^{i+1*}(.), \dots, p^{N*}(.)\} .$$

Let $\Sigma_i(C)$ be a game surface for player i, $\pi_i^*(C^*)$ a trajectory in R^{n+1} generated by $p^*(.)$ and emanating from $y^{i*}(0) \in \Sigma_i(C)$, and $\pi_i(C^i)$ a trajectory in R^{n+1} generated by $^ip(.)$ and emanating from $y^i(0) \in \Sigma_i(C)$. Then

(i) $\pi_i(C^i) \cap B/\Sigma_i(C) = \phi$, and

(ii) $\pi_i^*(C^*) \cap R^1 \times X^* \subset \Sigma_i(C)$ with $C^* = C$.

Proof. Let us first prove proposition (i) of the theorem. Let π denote the projection on R^n of $\pi_i(C^i)$ and let $y^{i'} = (x_o^{i'}, x')$ be a point on $\pi_i(C^i)$. Let $\bar{\pi}$ denote the portion of π that ends at x' and corresponds to solution $\bar{x}(.) : [0, \bar{\tau}_1] \to R^n$. Note that $y^{i'} \notin B/\Sigma_i(C^i)$ if $x' \notin X^*$, since $\Sigma_i(C)$ is defined on $R^1 \times X^*$. So suppose that $x' \in X^*$. Since we suppose that there exists an equilibrium strategy N-tuple on X, namely $p^*(.)$, we may consider a terminating solution $\bar{\bar{x}}(.) : [0, \bar{\bar{\tau}}_1] \to R^n$, $\bar{\bar{x}}(0) = x'$, with trajectory $\bar{\bar{\pi}}$, generated by $p^*(.)$.

In view of condition (iii) of Definition 2.2, there exists an admissible strategy N-tuple

$$^i\hat{p}(.) = \{p^{1*}(.), \dots, p^{i-1*}(.), \hat{p}^i(.), p^{i+1*}(.), \dots, p^{N*}(.)\}$$

with

$$\hat{p}^i(.) = p^i(.) \quad \text{for} \quad x_n \leqslant x_n'$$

$$\hat{p}^i(.) = p^{i*}(.) \quad \text{for} \quad x_n > x_n'$$

that generates a solution $\hat{x}^i(.) : [0, \hat{\tau}_1] \to R^n$, $\hat{x}^i(0) = x(0) = x^o$, with trajectory $\hat{\pi} = \bar{\pi} \cup \bar{\bar{\pi}}$; see Fig. 4.2. Let $V_i(x^o, {}^i\hat{p}(.), \hat{x}^i(.))$ denote the corresponding cost for player i.

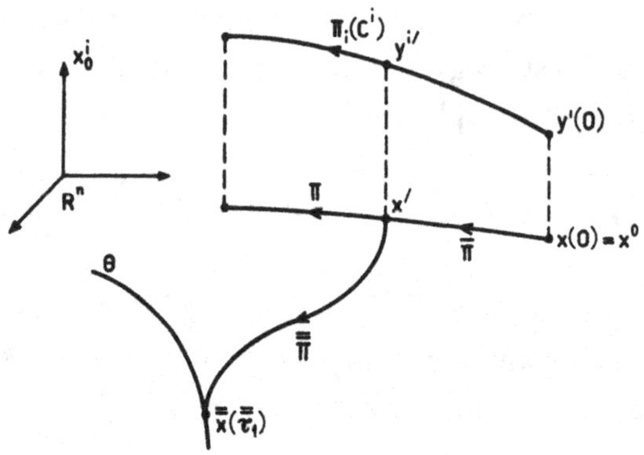

Fig. 4.2 Trajectories in proof of theorem 4.1

By (i) of Definition 4.1, we have

$$(4.15) \qquad V_i^*(x^o) = V_i(x^o, p^*(.), x^*(.)) \leqslant V_i(x^o, {}^i\hat{p}(.), \hat{x}^i(.))$$

where $x^*(.) : [0, \tau_1^*] \to R^n$, $x^*(0) = x^o$, is a terminating solution generated by $p^*(.)$. But

$$(4.16) \qquad V_i(x^o, {}^i\hat{p}(.), \hat{x}^i(.)) = V_i(x^o, {}^ip(.), \bar{x}(.)) + V_i(x', p^*(.), \bar{\bar{x}}(.))$$

where

$$(4.17) \qquad V_i(x', p^*(.), \bar{\bar{x}}(.)) = V_i^*(x')$$

Then, by (4.15) and (4.16),

$$V_i^*(x^\circ) - V_i^*(x') \leq V_i(x^\circ, {}^i p(.), \bar{x}(.)) \tag{4.18}$$

where, according to (4.5),

$$V_i(x^\circ, {}^i p(.), \bar{x}(.)) = x_0^{i'} - x_0^i(0) \tag{4.19}$$

But, since $y^i(0) \in \Sigma_i(C)$,

$$x_0^i(0) + V_i^*(x^\circ) = C \tag{4.20}$$

Then, on setting $y^i = y^{i'}$ in (4.13), relations (4.18) - (4.20) lead to

$$y^{i'} \in A/\Sigma_i'(C) \cup \Sigma_i(C).$$

Since $y^{i'}$ is any point of $\pi_i(C^i)$, that concludes the proof of proposition (i).

The second proposition follows at once from the definitions of $\pi_i^*(C^*)$ and $\Sigma_i(C)$. Suppose $p^*(.)$ generates a solution

$$y^{i*}(.) = (x_0^{i*}(.), x^*(.)) : [0, \tau_1] \to R^n,$$

$$y^{i*}(0) \in \Sigma_i(C) \quad \text{and} \quad x^*(0) = x^\circ,$$

with trajectory $\pi_i^*(C^*)$. From the definition of $\pi_i^*(C^*)$ it follows that

$$x_0^{i*}(\tau) + V_i^*(x^*(\tau)) = C^* \tag{4.21}$$

But $y^{i*}(0) \in \Sigma_i(C)$ implies

$$x_0^{i*}(0) + V_i^*(x^\circ) = C \tag{4.22}$$

From (4.21) and (4.22) we have at once that $C^* = C$. Then, on letting $x = x^*(\tau)$ in (4.12), we have $x_0^i = x_0^{i*}(\tau)$. This concludes the proof.

Theorem 4.1 expresses a fundamental property of game surfaces. In order to permit us to utilize this property for the deduction of necessary conditions, we shall make assumptions which restrict the class of equilibrium strategy N-tuples.

4.3. Regular Optimal Trajectories : Necessary Conditions for an Equilibrium.

Before proceeding to a derivation of necessary conditions, we need

Definition 4.5. Let $p^*(.)$ be an equilibrium strategy N-tuple on X, which generates an optimal solution $y^{i*}(.) : [0, \tau_1^*] \to R^{n+1}$ with corresponding trajectory $\pi_i^*(C)$ whose projection on R^n is π^*. Trajectory $\pi^*(C)$ is regular if and only if

(i) all points of π^*, with the possible exception of terminal point $x^*(\tau_1^*)$, belong to the interior of X^*,

(ii) every point of π^*, with the possible exception of terminal point $x^*(\tau_1^*)$, possesses a neighborhood in R^n on which $V_i^*(.)$ is of class C^2,

(iii) every point of π^* possesses a neighborhood in R^n on which $p^*(.)$ is of class C^1, and

(iv)(*) for all $x \in \pi^*$ and $u^i \in U^i(x)$ there exists a strategy $p_x^i(.)$ that is of class C^1 on a neighborhood in R^n of x and such that $p_x^i(x) = u^i$ and strategy N-tuple ${}^ip(.) = \{p^{1*}(.),\dots,p^{i-1*}(.),p_x^i(.),p^{i+1*}(.),\dots,p^{N*}(.)\}$ is admissible.

Now consider a point $y^i = (x_0^i, x) \in \pi_i^*(C)$, $y^i = y^{i*}(\tau)$, $\tau < \tau_1^*$ By (i) of Definition 4.5, y^i is an interior point of $R^1 \times X^*$. Next consider a strategy N-tuple

$$ {}^ip(.) = \{p^{1*}(.),\dots,p^{i-1*}(.),p_x^i(.),p^{i+1*}(.),\dots,p^{N*}(.)\} \in P $$

with $p_x^i(x) = u^i \in U^i(x)$, which generates a solution $y^i(.) : [0,\tau_1] \to R^{n+1}$, $y^i(0) = y^i$, with corresponding trajectory $\pi_i(C^i)$ Such a solution exists in view of (iv) of Definition 4.5. Since $y^i \in \pi_i^*(C)$ is an interior point of $R^1 \times X^*$ it follows at once from Theorem 4.1. that

$$ (4.23) \qquad \pi_i(C^i) \subset A/\Sigma_i(C) \cup \Sigma_i(C) $$

for sufficiently small τ_1, and

$$ (4.24) \qquad \pi_i^*(C) \subset \Sigma_i(C) $$

We now recall the function $\Phi_i(.)$ defined by (4.14). As a consequence of (ii) of Definition 4.5, function $\Phi_i(.)$ is of class C^2 on $R^1 \times X^*$. Consequently, relations (4.23) and (4.24) result in

$$ \text{4.25)} \qquad \begin{aligned} &\operatorname{grad} \Phi_i(y^i) g^i(y^i, {}^ip(x)) \geq 0 \qquad \forall u^i \in U^i(x) \\ &\operatorname{grad} \Phi_i(y^i) g^i(y^i, p^*(x)) = 0 \end{aligned} $$

(*) If $U^i(x) = \text{constant} \ \forall\, x \in X^*$, this condition is satisfied.

for all $y^i \in \pi_i^*(C)$, $y^i \notin Ⓗ$, where

$$\operatorname{grad} \Phi_i(y^i) = \left(1, \frac{\partial V_i^*(x)}{\partial x_1}, \dots, \frac{\partial V_i^*(x)}{\partial x_n}\right).$$

According to (i) of Definition 4.5, point $y^i = y^{i*}(\tau)$, $\tau < \tau_1^*$, is an interior point of $R^1 \times X^*$, and hence possesses a neighborhood all of whose points belong to optimal trajectories. Consequently, the second of relations (4.25) is valid at every point of such a neighborhood. so that it is an identity in y^i; thus, it can be differentiated with respect to y^i. This is allowed because of (ii) and (iii) of Definition 4.5.

Omitting the arguments for the sake of brevity, let

$$\frac{d^2\Phi_i}{dy^{i2}} = \begin{bmatrix} 0 & 0 & \cdots & 0 \\ 0 & \frac{\partial^2 V_i^*}{\partial x_1^2} & \cdots & \frac{\partial^2 V_i^*}{\partial x_1 \partial x_n} \\ \vdots & & & \vdots \\ 0 & \frac{\partial^2 V_i^*}{\partial x_n \partial x_1} & \cdots & \frac{\partial^2 V_i^*}{\partial x_n^2} \end{bmatrix}$$

$$\frac{\partial g^i}{\partial y^i} = \begin{bmatrix} 0 & \frac{\partial f_o^i}{\partial x_1} & \cdots & \frac{\partial f_o^i}{\partial x_n} \\ \vdots & & & \vdots \\ 0 & \frac{\partial f_n}{\partial x_1} & \cdots & \frac{\partial f_n}{\partial x_n} \end{bmatrix}$$

$$\frac{\partial g^i}{\partial u} = \begin{bmatrix} \frac{\partial f_o^i}{\partial u_1} & \frac{\partial f_o^i}{\partial u_2} & \cdots & \frac{\partial f_o^i}{\partial u_K} \\ \vdots & & & \vdots \\ \frac{\partial f_n}{\partial u_1} & \frac{\partial f_n}{\partial u_2} & \cdots & \frac{\partial f_n}{\partial u_K} \end{bmatrix}$$

$$\frac{dp^*}{dy^i} = \begin{bmatrix} 0 & \frac{\partial p_1^*}{\partial x_1} & \cdots & \frac{\partial p_1^*}{\partial x_n} \\ \vdots & & & \vdots \\ 0 & \frac{\partial p_K^*}{\partial x_1} & \cdots & \frac{\partial p_K^*}{\partial x_n} \end{bmatrix}$$

all evaluated at $y^i = y^{i*}(\tau)$, $u^i = p^{i*}(x^*(\tau))$.

Differentiation of the second relation of (4.25) results in

$$\frac{d^2\Phi_i}{dy^{i2}} g^i(y^i, p^*(x)) + \left[\frac{\partial g^i}{\partial y^i} + \frac{\partial g^i}{\partial u}\frac{dp^*}{dy^i}\right]^T \mathrm{grad}^T \Phi_i(y^i) = 0$$

(4.26).

Now introduce function

$$\lambda^i(.): [0,\tau_1^*] \to R^{n+1}$$

such that

$$\lambda^i(\tau) = \mathrm{grad}^T \Phi_i(y^{i*}(\tau)) \tag{4.27}$$

for all $\tau \in [0,\tau_1^*)$. Thus, in view of (4.26) and

$$\frac{\partial^2 V_i^*}{\partial x_j \partial x_k} = \frac{\partial^2 V_i^*}{\partial x_k \partial x_j} \quad \text{at } y^{i*}(\tau), \quad \tau < \tau_1^*,$$

function $\lambda^i(.)$ is a solution of

$$\dot{\lambda}^i(\tau) = -\left[\frac{\partial g^i}{\partial y^i} + \frac{\partial g^i}{\partial u}\frac{dp^*}{dy^i}\right]^T \lambda^i(\tau) \tag{4.28}$$

Since the solution of (4.28) is defined and continuous on $[0,\tau_1^*]$,

$$\lim_{\substack{\tau \to \tau_1^* \\ \tau < \tau_1^*}} \mathrm{grad}^T \Phi_i(y^{i*}(\tau)) = \lambda^i(\tau_1^*) \tag{4.29}$$

Note also that the right-hand side of (4.28) is independent of x_o^i so that, as expected, $\lambda_o^i(\tau) \equiv$ constant; in view of (4.27)

$$\lambda_o^i(\tau) \equiv 1 \tag{4.30}$$

Next we introduce function

$$H^i(.) : R^{n+1} \times R^1 \times X \times R^K \to R^1$$

such that

$$H^i(\lambda^i, y^i, u) = \lambda^{iT} g^i(y^i, u) \tag{4.31}$$

In terms of the H^i-function. conditions (4.25) can be rewritten as

$$\min_{u^i \in U^i(x)} H^i(\lambda^i(\tau), y^{i*}(\tau), {}^i p(x^*(\tau))) =$$

$$= H^i(\lambda^i(\tau), y^{i*}(\tau), p^*(x^*(\tau))) = 0 \tag{4.32}$$

for all $\tau \in [0, \tau_1^*)$, where

$${}^i p(x) = \{p^{1*}(x), \ldots, p^{i-1*}(x), u^i, p^{i+1*}(x), \ldots, p^{N*}(x)\} .$$

Now consider the function

$$\mathcal{H}^i(.) : [0, \tau_1^*] \to R^1$$

such that

$$\mathcal{H}^i(\tau) = H^i(\lambda^i(\tau), y^{i*}(\tau), {}^i p(x^*(\tau))) \tag{4.33}$$

Since $g^i(\cdot)$ and $p^*(.)$ are of class C^1, and $\lambda^i(.)$ and $y^{i*}(.)$ are continuous, $\mathcal{H}^i(.)$ is continuous on $[0, \tau_1^*]$ if ${}^i p(.) = p^*(.)$; hence, the second of (4.32) holds on $[0, \tau_1^*]$. To show that the first of (4.32) is also valid on the closed interval, consider condition (iv) of Definition (4.5). Namely, consider a strategy $p^i(\cdot) = p_x^i(\cdot)$, $x = x^*(\tau_1^*)$, of class C^1 on a neighborhood of $x^*(\tau_1^*)$, such that

$$p_x^i(x) = u^i \in U^i(x) \quad \text{for} \quad x = x^*(\tau_1^*)$$

Then there exists an $\epsilon > 0$ such that

$$\mathcal{H}^i(\tau) = \lambda^{iT}(\tau) g^i(y^{i*}(\tau), {}^i p(x^*(\tau))) \geq 0$$

for $\tau \in [\tau_1^* - \epsilon, \tau_1^*)$ and $\mathcal{H}^i(.)$ is continuous on $[\tau_1^* - \epsilon, \tau_1^*]$. Thus, the first of (4.32) holds also at $\tau = \tau_1^*$.

Next we turn to a condition that must be satisfied at the terminal point, $y^{i*}(\tau_1^*)$, of a regular optimal trajectory, π_i^* (C). Since grad $\Phi_i(y^i)$ is defined on a neighborhood of $y^{i*}(\tau)$, $\tau \in [0, \tau_1^*)$, the tangent plane of $\Sigma_i(C)$, $T_\Sigma(y^{i*}(\tau))$, is defined at $y^{i*}(\tau)$, $\tau \in [0, \tau_1^*)$; its normal is in the direction of grad $\Phi_i(y^{i*}(\tau))$. Since a unique trajectory π_i^* (C) passes through $y^{i*}(\tau_1^*)$(*) and as a consequence of (4.29), that normal and hence the tangent plane are defined at $y^{i*}(\tau_1^*)$.

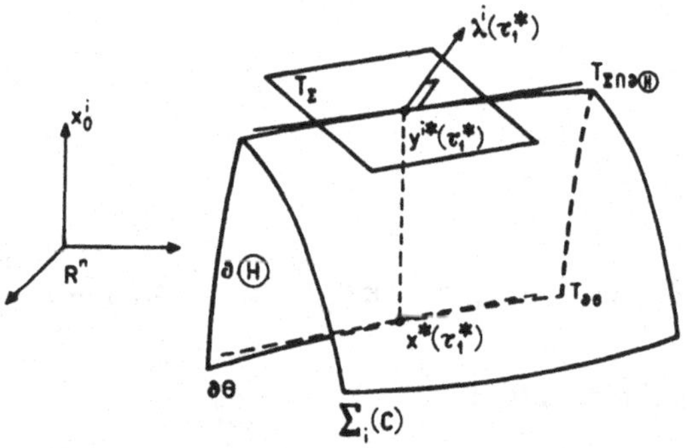

Fig. 4.3 Transversality conditions

The set (**)

$$\Sigma_i(C) \cap Ⓗ = \{y^i : x_0^i = C, \ x \in \theta\}$$

is deduced from θ by translation parallel to the x_0^i -axis. Since $\partial\theta$ possesses a tangent

(*) Recall that $p^*(.)$ is C^1 in neigborhood of $x^*(\tau_1^*)$.

(**) Recall (4.1)

plane, $T_{\partial\theta}(x)$, for all $x \in \partial\theta$, so does $\Sigma_i(C) \cap \partial Ⓗ$; let it be denoted by $T_{\Sigma\cap\partial Ⓗ}(y^i)$. This latter tangent plane is deduced from $T_{\partial\theta}(x)$ by translation parallel to the x_o^i -axis. Since

$$T_{\Sigma\cap\partial Ⓗ}(y^i) \subset T_{\Sigma}(y^i)$$

and since $\lambda^i(\tau_1^*)$ is normal to $T_{\Sigma}(y^{i*}(\tau_1^*))$, it follows that $\lambda^i(\tau_1^*)$ is normal to $T_{\Sigma\cap\partial Ⓗ}(y^{i*}(\tau_1^*))$. This is the terminal transversality condition. It can be expressed as follows. Let $\eta \in R^{n+1}$ be a vector in $T_{\Sigma\cap\partial Ⓗ}(y^{i*}(\tau_1^*))$. Then

$$\lambda^{iT}(\tau_1^*)\ \eta = 0 \tag{4.34}$$

for all such η; namely, (4.34) must hold for all η such that

$$\begin{aligned} \eta_o &= 0 \\ \sum_{i=1}^{n} \frac{\partial\theta(x^*(\tau_1^*))}{\partial x_i}\ \eta_i &= 0 \end{aligned} \tag{4.35}$$

Relation (4.34), together with (4.35), yields n-1 conditions at $\tau = \tau_1^*$, in addition to terminal condition

$$\theta(x^*(\tau_1^*)) = 0 \tag{4.36}$$

Thus, the problem of integrating the state equation and eq. (4.28), not including the zeroth component of the latter. is well posed.

The results of this section can be summarized in

Theorem 4.2. If $p^*(\cdot)$ is a Nash equilibrium on $X \subset R^n$, which generates a regular optimal trajectory $\pi_i^*(C)$, $i \in \{1,2,..N\}$, corresponding to solution $y^{i*}(.) = (x_o^{i*}(.),\ x^*(\cdot)) : [0,\tau_1^*] \to R^{n+1}$, then there exists a solution $\lambda^i(.) : [0,\tau_1^*] \to R^{n+1}$ of (4.28) such that

(a)
$$\min_{u^i \in U^i(x^*(\tau))} H^i(\lambda^i(\tau), y^{i*}(\tau), {}^i p(x^*(\tau))) = H^i(\lambda^i(\tau), y^{i*}(\tau), p^*(x^*(\tau))) = 0,$$

(b)
$$\lambda_o^i(\tau) = 1$$

for all $\tau \in [0,\tau_1^*]$, and

(c) transversality condition is satisfied.

Note that (4.28) may be written in component form as

$$\dot{\lambda}^i_j(\tau) = -\frac{\partial H^i(\lambda^i, y^i, u)}{\partial x_j} - \sum_{k=1}^{K} \frac{\partial H^i(\lambda^i, y^i, u)}{\partial u_k} \frac{\partial p^*_k(x)}{\partial x_j} \qquad (4.37)$$

$$j = 0, 1, \dots, n$$

where $\lambda^i = \lambda^i(\tau)$, $y^i = y^{i*}(\tau)$, $u = p^*(x^*(\tau))$.
Of course

$$\dot{\lambda}^i_0(\tau) = 0$$

4.4. Piecewise Regular Optimal Trajectories: Necessary Conditions for an Equilibrium.

The conditions of Theorem 4.2 can be somewhat generalized by relaxing the conditions imposed in Definition 4.5. To do so we need

Definition 4.6. Let X be a domain (open connected set) of R^n. $\{X_1, X_2, X_L\}$ is a finite decomposition of X if and only if

(i) X_i, i = 1, 2, ..., L, is a domain of R^n,
(ii) $X_i \cap X_j = \phi$ for $i \neq j$,
(iii) $X_i \subseteq X$, $i = 1, 2, \dots, L$, and
(iv) $X \subset \bigcup_{i=1}^{L} \overline{X}_i$.

As a consequence of the conditions of Definition 4.6,

$$\overline{X} = \bigcup_{i=1}^{L} \overline{X}_i$$

Definition 4.7. Given a game surface $\Sigma_i(C)$ and a finite decomposition of domain X, $\{\Sigma_i^1(C), \Sigma_i^2(C), \dots, \Sigma_i^L(C)\}$ is a finite decomposition of $\Sigma_i(C)$ if and only if

$$\Sigma^j_i(C) = \{y^i : \Phi_i(y^i) = C, \quad x \in X_j\} \qquad \text{for } j \in \{1, 2, \dots, L\}.$$

Now we introduce the following

Assumptions.

(i) (*) Set X is a domain of R^n with a finite decomposition $\{X_1, X_2, ..., X_L\}$ such that $p^*(,)$ agrees on each X_i with a function, say $p_{X_i}(\cdot)$, of class C^1 on a domain $R_i \supset X_i$, and on each non-empty $M_{ij} = \overline{X}_i \cap \overline{X}_j$, $i \neq j$, with a function, say $p_{M_{ij}}(\cdot)$, of class C^1 on a domain $R_{ij} \supset M_{ij}$.

(ii) Each discontinuity manifold M_{ij} is a smooth (n - 1)-dimensional surface; that is

$$x \in M_{ij} \Rightarrow m_{ij}(x) = 0$$

where $m_{ij}(.): R_{ij} \to R^1$ is of class C^1 and grad $m_{ij}(x) \neq 0$ for $x \in R_{ij}$.

(iii) Each $V_i^*(.)$ is continuous on X and agrees on each X_j with a function, say $V_i^j(.)$, of class C^2 on a domain $R_j \supset X_j$.

By methods similar to those employed in the derivation of Theorem 4.2, one arrives at

Theorem 4.3. If $p^*(.)$ is a Nash equilibrium on a domain $X \subseteq R^n$, which generates a solution $y^{i*}(.) = (x_0^{i*}(.), x^*(.)) : [0, \tau_1^*] \to R^{n+1}$, $i \in \{1, 2, ..., N\}$, and if Assumptions (i) - (iii) are met, then on every interval $[\tau_\alpha, \tau_\beta] \subseteq [0, \tau_1^*]$ such that $y^{i*}(\tau) \in R^1 \times X_j$, $j \in \{1, 2, ..., L\}$, for $\tau \in (\tau_\alpha, \tau_\beta)$, there exists a solution $\lambda^i(.) : [\tau_\alpha, \tau_\beta] \to R^{n+1}$ of (4.28) such that

(a)
$$\underset{u^i \in U^i(x^*(\tau))}{\mathrm{Min}} H^i(\lambda^i(\tau), y^{i*}(\tau), {}^i p(x^*(\tau))) =$$
$$= H^i(\lambda^i(\tau), y^{i*}(\tau), p^*(x^*(\tau))) = 0$$

(b)
$$\lambda_0^i(\tau) = 1$$

for all $\tau \in [\tau_\alpha, \tau_\beta]$, and if there is an $\epsilon > 0$ such that $x^*(\tau) \in X_j$, $j \in \{1, 2, ..., L\}$, for $\tau \in [\tau_1^* - \epsilon, \tau_1^*)$,

(c) (**) transversality condition is satisfied.

One can derive other necessary conditions. For instance, one can give a

---

(*) Note that X* need not be a domain; for example, see Sec. 5.5

(**) That is, if the trajectory approaches the target from the interior of a member of the decomposition.

"jump condition" for trajectories which cross discontinuity manifolds; this condition relates the left and right limits of $\lambda^i(\tau)$ at a point of an M_{ij} where a trajectory crosses from X_i into X_j. One can also classify some types of discontinuity manifolds (singular surfaces). For these and related matters, see Ref. 4.7 - 4.11.

So far we have discussed necessary conditions for a Nash equilibrium. Next we shall take up sufficient conditions.

4.5 Sufficient Conditions for an Equilibrium

Since Ref. 4.12 devotes an entire chapter to various sufficiency theorems for Nash equilibria in differential games, we shall deal only briefly with sufficient conditions. It is possible to give sufficiency theorems analogous to theorems 3.1, 3.4 and 3.5. Here we shall state, again without proof (see Ref. 4.12), a theorem analogous to Theorem 3.5.

Theorem 4.4. A strategy N - tuple $p^*(.)$ that is playable for all $x^o \in X$ is an equilibrium on X with respect to every strategy N - tuple $p(.)$ that is playable at $x^o \in X$ and whose terminating solutions $x(.) : [0,\tau_1] \to R^n$ are such that $x(\tau) \in X$ for all $\tau \in [0,\tau_1]$, if there exists a denumerable decomposition D of X and for each $i \in \{1, 2, ..., N\}$ there exists a continuous function $V^i(.) : X \to R^1$ that is continuously differentiable with respect to D such that for all $x^o \in X$

(i) $\int_0^{\tau_1^*} f_0^i(x^*(\tau), p^*(x^*(\tau)))\,d\tau = V^i(x^o)$,

for all terminating solutions $x^*(.)$ generated by $p^*(.)$,

(ii) $f_0^i(x, p^{1*}(x), ..., p^{i-1*}(x), u^i, p^{i+1*}(x), ..., p^{N*}(x))$

$+ \operatorname{grad} V_j^i(x) f(x, p^{1*}(x), ..., p^{i-1*}(x), u^i, p^{i+1*}(x), ..., p^{N*}(x)) \geqslant 0$

for all $x \in X_j$, $u^i \in U^i(x)$, $j \in J$, where $\{(W_j, V_j^i) : j \in J\}$ is a collection associated with $V^i(.)$ and $D = \{X_j : j \in J\}$ for each $i \in \{1, 2, ..., N\}$, and

(iii) $V^i(x) = 0$ for all $x \in \theta$.

Other sufficiency theorems can be found in Refs. 4.3, 4.12 and 4.13.

4.6 Example: Collective Bargaining

Here we consider again the problem of negotiation between management and union during a strike as posed in Section 3.4. There we sought and obtained Pareto-optimal control N - tulpes, treating the problem as a cooperative game. Here we shall treat the same problem as a non-cooperative game and seek a Nash equilibrium; the only change in the problem will be in the absence of constraints on the values of the strategies. Thus, we have state equation(*)

$$\dot{z}(\tau) = -[u(\tau)+v(\tau)]z(\tau) \tag{4.38}$$

where

$$u(\tau) = p^1(z(\tau)) \in R^1$$

$$v(\tau) = p^2(z(\tau)) \in R^1$$

The initial state

$$z(0) = z^\circ \in [m,\infty)$$

and the target set

$$\theta = \{z : z - m = 0\} \tag{4.39}$$

The costs are

$$\begin{aligned} V_1(z^\circ, p(.), z(.)) &= \int_0^{\tau_1} [k_1 + u(\tau)z(\tau)]d\tau \\ V_2(z^\circ, p(.), z(.)) &= \int_0^{\tau_1} [k_2 + v(\tau)z(\tau)]d\tau \end{aligned} \tag{4.40}$$

We seek a strateg pair $p^*(.) = \{p^{1*}(.), p^{2*}(.)\}$ that is a Nash equilibrium on $[m,\infty)$.

Now it is readily verified that $p^*(.)$ given by

$$p^{1*}(z) = \frac{k_2}{z}, \quad p^{2*}(z) = \frac{k_1}{z} \tag{4.41}$$

is a candidate in that it satisfies the necessary conditions embodied in Theorem 4.2.

First of all, we find that for $p^*(.)$ given by (4.41)

$$\dot{\lambda}^i(\tau) = 0 \qquad i = 1,2$$

and that condition (c), the transversality condition, is met for arbitrary $\overset{i}{\lambda}(\tau_1^*)$.

(*) Again, there is no need to consider time, t, as a state component.

Condition (a) can be satisfied by

$$\lambda^i(\tau) \equiv 1 \qquad i = 1,2$$

upon use of condition (b). Thus, the conditions of Theorem 4.2 are fulfilled. It remains to demonstrate that p*(.) is indeed an equilibrium. To do so we invoke Theorem 4.4.

No decomposition is needed. It is easily shown, on integration of (4.40), that

$$V_i(z^o, p^*(.), z^*(.)) = (k_1 + k_2)\tau_1^* \qquad i = 1,2$$

and, on integration of (4.38), that

$$\tau_1^* = \frac{z^o - m}{k_1 + k_2}$$

Thus, we shall choose

$$V^i(z) = z - m \qquad i = 1,2$$

With this choice of the $V^i(.)$, the conditions of Theorem 4.4 are trivially met. And so p*(.) is indeed a Nash equilibrium.

A cautionary note is in order. While we have deduced a Nash equilibrium, we have not shown that it is unique. Nonetheless. the particular Nash equilibrium obtained here is of special interest because it results in bargaining (offer and demand rates, $\dot{x}(\tau)$ and $\dot{y}(\tau)$) that does not depend on the current state of the negotiation.

References for Chapter 4

[4.1] Ciletti, M.D., Differential Games with Information Time Lag, in Topics in Differential Games (ed. E. Blaquière, A.), North Holland, Amsterdam, 1973.

[4.2] Blaquière, A., Differential Games with Time Lag, in Techniques of Optimization (ed. Balakrishnan, A.V.) Academic Press, N.Y., 1972.

[4.3] Case, J.H., Toward a Theory of Many Player Differential Games, SIAM J. Control, Vol. 7, No. 2, 1969.

[4.4] Leitmann, G. Differential Games, in Differential Games: Theory and Applications (eds. Ciletti, M.D. and Starr, A.W.), ASME, N.Y., 1970

[4.5] Ho, Y.C. and Starr, A.W., Nonzero-Sum Differential Games, J. Optim. Theory Appl., Vol. 3, No. 3, 1969.

[4.6] Ho, Y.C. and Starr, A.W., Further Properties of Nonzero-Sum Differential Games, J. Optim. Theory Appl., Vol. 3, No. 4, 1969.

[4.7] Isaacs, R., Differential Games, Wiley, N.Y., 1965.

[4.8] Berkovitz, L.D., Necessary Conditions for Optimal Strategies in a Class of Differential Games and Control Problems, SIAM J. Control, Vol. 5, No. 1, 1967.

[4.9] Blaquière, A., Gérard, F., and Leitmann, G., Quantitative and Qualitative Games, Academic Press, N.Y., 1969.

[4.10] Leitmann, G. and Mon, G., On a Class of Differential Games, in Advanced Problems and Methods for Space Flight Optimization (ed. Fraeijs de Veubecke) Pergamon, N.Y., 1969.

[4.11] Blaquière, A. and Leitmann, G., Jeux Quantitatifs, Gauthier-Villars, Paris, 1969

[4.12] Stalford, H. and Leitmann, G. Sufficiency Conditions for Nash Equilibria in N-Person Differential Games, in Topics in Differential Games (ed. A. Blaquière), North-Holland, Amsterdam, 1973.

[4.13] Leitmann, G. and Stalford, H., Sufficiency for Optimal Strategies in Nash Equilibrium Games, in Techniques of Optimization (ed. A. V. Balakrishnan), Academic Press, N.Y., 1971.

5. Two-Person Zero-Sum Games

5.1 Saddle-Point

As discussed in Section 1.3, two-person zero-sum games constitute an important class of Nash equilibrium games. Differential games of this class have been extensively treated, for instance in Refs. 5.1 5.4; here we shall only give those results which arise directly from specializing the N-person nonzero-sum case. Before doing so let us note that (1.5) becomes

$$V_1(.) = -V_2(.) = V(.) \tag{5.1}$$

that is,

$$\begin{aligned} f_o^1(.) &= -f_o^2(.) = f_o(.) \\ x_o^1(.) &= -x_o^2(.) = x_o(.) \end{aligned} \tag{5.2}$$

Then Definition 1.3 becomes

Definition 5.1. A strategy pair $p^*(.) = \{p^{1*}(.), p^{2*}(.)\}$ is a <u>saddle-point</u> on a set $X \subseteq R^n$ if and only if

(i) it is playable at all $x^o \epsilon X$, and

(ii) $V(x^o; {}^2p(.), x^2(.)) \leqslant V(x^o; p^*(.), x^*(.)) \leqslant V(x^o; {}^1p(.), x^1(.))$

for all terminating $\{x^o; {}^ip(.), x^i(.)\}$, $i=1,2$, $\{x^o; p^*(.), x^*(.)\}$, and all $x^o \epsilon X$.

This definition corresponds to Definition 4.1 for nonzero-sum games. Note that condition (iii) of the latter definition is not imposed here, it is already implied by condition (ii). In other words, if there are two terminating plays, $\{x^o, p^*(.), x^*(.)\}$ and $\{x^o, p^*(.), x^{**}(.)\}$, condition (ii) implies the equality of the corresponding costs. Again, we note that the conditions of Definition 5.1 hold trivially for $x^o \epsilon\, \theta$. Thus, for given saddle-point, $p^*(.)$, we can define

$$V^*(.) : X^* = X \cup \theta \rightarrow R^1$$

such that

$$V^*(x^o) = V(x^o; p^*(.), x^*(.))$$

for all terminating plays $\{x^o, p^*(.), x^*(.)\}$ and all $x^o \epsilon X^*$.

Before turning to a derivation of necessary conditions, a few words concerning the special properties of two-person zero-sum games are in order. These are embodied in Lemmas 1.3 - 1.5.

Lemmas 1.3 and 1.4 have ready counterparts for differential games. Lemma 1.3 becomes

Lemma 5.1. If both $\{p^{1*}(.), p^{2*}(.)\}$ and $\{\hat{p}^1(.), \hat{p}^2(.)\}$ are saddle-points on X and if, given $x^o \epsilon X$, $\{x^o, p^{1*}(.), p^{2*}(.), x^*(.)\}$ and $\{x^o, \hat{p}^1(.), \hat{p}^2(.), \hat{x}(.)\}$ are terminating plays, then

$$V(x^o, p^{1*}(.), p^{2*}(.), x^*(.)) = V(x^o, \hat{p}^1(.), \hat{p}^2(.), \hat{x}(.)).$$

Lemma 1.4 becomes

Lemma 5.2. If both $\{p^{1*}(.), p^{2*}(.)\}$ and $\{\hat{p}^1(.), \hat{p}^2(.)\}$ are saddle-points on X, and if both $\{p^1(.), \hat{p}^2(.)\}$ and $\{\hat{p}^1(.), p^{2*}(.)\}$ are playable at all $x^o \epsilon X$, then $\{p^{1*}(.), \hat{p}^2(.)\}$ and $\{\hat{p}^1(.), p^{2*}(.)\}$ are also saddle-points on X.

On the other hand, Lemma 1.5 has no direct analog for differential games. However, if there exist sets of strategies, P^1 and P^2, such that

(i) $P^1 x P^2 = P$, and

(ii) given $x^o \epsilon X$, $\overset{1}{p}(.) \epsilon \overset{1}{P}$, $\overset{2}{p}(.) \epsilon \overset{2}{P}$, there is a unique terminating solution, x(.),

then one can identify d_i with $\overset{i}{p}(.)$ and D_i with $\overset{i}{P}$, so that Lemma 1.5 applies directly. An example of such behavior <u>may</u> (*) be found in so-called "linear-quadratic" games; for example, see Ref. 5.5.

5.2 Necessary Conditions for a Saddle-Point

The necessary conditions embodied in Theorems 4.2 and 4.3 can be recast easily to fit the two-person zero-sum situation. To do so, we note that

$$\Phi_1(y^1) = -\Phi_2(y^2) = \Phi(y) \tag{5.3}$$

where $y = (x_o, x)$. Consequently,

$$\lambda^1(\tau) = -\lambda^2(\tau) = \lambda(\tau) \tag{5.4}$$

and

$$\begin{aligned} H^1(\lambda^1, y^1, u) &= -H^2(\lambda^2, y^2, u) \\ &= H(\lambda, y, u^1, u^2) \\ &= \lambda^T g(y, u^1, u^2) \end{aligned} \tag{5.5}$$

(*) For instance by further restricting admissible strategies to the class of linear functions of the x_i, $i = 1, 2, ..., n-1$,

where $g(.) = (f_o(.), f(.))$.

Then, eqs. (4.37) become

$$\dot{\lambda}_j(\tau) = -\frac{\partial H(\lambda, y, u^1, u^2)}{\partial x_j} - \sum_{i=1}^{d_1} \frac{\partial H(\lambda, y, u^1, u^2)}{\partial u_i^1} \frac{\partial p_i^{1*}(x)}{\partial x_j} - \sum_{i=1}^{d_2} \frac{\partial H(\lambda, y, u^1, u^2)}{\partial u_i^2} \frac{\partial p_i^{2*}(x)}{\partial x_j} \tag{5.6}$$

$$j = 0, 1, \ldots, n$$

where $\lambda = \lambda(\tau)$, $y = y^*(\tau)$, $u^i = p^{i*}(x^*(\tau))$.

Again, of course

$$\dot{\lambda}_o(\tau) = 0$$

Now we are ready to state the counterpart to Theorem 4.2.

Theorem 5.1. If $\{p^{1*}(.), p^{2*}(.)\}$ is a saddle-point on $X \subseteq R^n$, which generates a regular optimal trajectory $\pi^*(C)$, corresponding to solution $y^*(.) = (x_o^*(.), x^*(.)) : [0, \tau_1^*] \to R^{n+1}$, then there exists a solution $\lambda(.) : [0, \tau_1^*] \to R^{n+1}$ of (5.6) such that

(a)
$$\min_{u^1 \in U^1(x^*(\tau))} H(\lambda(\tau), y^*(\tau), u^1, p^{2*}(x^*(\tau))) = \max_{u^2 \in U^2(x^*(\tau))} H(\lambda(\tau), y^*(\tau), p^{1*}(x^*(\tau)), u^2) = 0,$$

(b) $\lambda_o(\tau) = 1$

for all $\tau \in [0, \tau_1^*]$, and

(c) the transversality condition is satisfied.

On the other hand, Theorem 4.3 becomes

Theorem 5.2. If $\{p^{1*}(.), p^{2*}(.)\}$ is a saddle-point on a domain $X \subseteq R^n$, which generates a solution $\overset{*}{y}(.) = (x_0^*(.), x^*(.)) : [0, \tau_1^*] \to R^{n+1}$, and if Assumptions (i)-(iii) are met, then on every interval $[\tau_\alpha, \tau_\beta] \subseteq [0, \overset{*}{\tau_1}]$ such that $y^*(\tau) \in R^1 x X_j$, $j \in \{1, 2, ..., L\}$, for $(\tau_\alpha, \tau_\beta)$, there exists a solution $\lambda^i(.) : [\tau_\alpha, \tau_\beta] \to R^{n+1}$ of (5.6) such that

(a)
$$\min_{u^1 \in U^1(x^*(\tau))} H(\lambda(\tau), y^*(\tau), u^1, p^{2*}(x^*(\tau))) =$$

$$= \max_{u^2 \in U^2(x^*(\tau))} H(\lambda(\tau), y^*(\tau), p^{1*}(x^*(\tau)), u^2) = 0,$$

(b) $\lambda_0(\tau) = 1$

for all $\tau \in [\tau_\alpha, \tau_\beta]$, and if there is an $\epsilon > 0$ such that $x^*(\tau) \in X_j$, $j \in \{1, 2, ..., L\}$, for $\tau \in [\tau_1^* - \epsilon, \tau_1^*)$,

(c) transversality condition is satisfied.

5.3 Constraints

A further simplification, unique to two-person zero-sum games, can be effected if the constraint function $U^i(.)$ satisfy certain conditions.

Suppose that $U^1(x)$ and $U^2(x)$ are defined by

(5.7)
$$\varphi_i(x, u^1) \leq 0 \qquad i = 1, 2, ..., k$$
$$\psi_i(x, u^2) \leq 0 \qquad i = 1, 2, ..., \ell$$

respectively, where

$$\varphi_i(.) : R^n x R^{d_1} \to R^1$$
$$\psi_i(.) : R^n x R^{d_2} \to R^1$$

are of class C^1.

Suppose further that

(5.8) (*)
$$\varphi_i(x, p^{1*}(x)) = 0 \qquad i = 1, 2, ..., k' \leq k$$
$$\psi_i(x, p^{2*}(x)) = 0 \qquad i = 1, 2, ..., \ell' \leq \ell$$

at $x = x^*(\tau)$.

(*) If necessary by relabelling.

We shall assume that, if $k > d_1$ or $\ell > d_2$, at most d_1 of the $\varphi_1(x, u^1)$ or d_2 of the $\psi_i(x, u^2)$ vanish at any point of $R^n \times R^{d_1}$ or $R^n \times R^{d_2}$, respectively, and furthermore that the matrices

$$\left[\frac{\partial \varphi_i\,(x,u^1)}{\partial u_j^1}\right] \qquad \begin{array}{l} i = 1,2,\ldots,k' \\ j = 1,2,\ldots,d_1 \end{array}$$

$$\left[\frac{\partial \psi_i\,(x,u^2)}{\partial u_j^2}\right] \qquad \begin{array}{l} i = 1,2,\ldots,\ell' \\ j = 1,2,\ldots,d_2 \end{array}$$

have maximum rank at $x = x^*(\tau)$, $u^i = p^{i*}(x^*(\tau))$.

Now, by the multiplier rule, condition (a) of Theorem 5.1 and 5.2 implies that there exist

$$\begin{array}{llll} \mu \in R^k, \text{ with } \mu_i & \geqslant 0 \,, & i = 1,2,\ldots,k' \\ \phantom{\mu \in R^k, \text{ with }} \mu_i & = 0 \,, & i = k'+1, k'+2,\ldots, k \\ \nu \in R^\ell, \text{ with } \nu_i & \leqslant 0 \,, & i = 1,2,\ldots,\ell' \\ \phantom{\nu \in R^\ell, \text{ with }} \nu_i & = 0 \,, & i = \ell'+1, \ell'+2,\ldots, \ell \end{array}$$

such that

$$\begin{aligned} \frac{\partial H}{\partial u^1} + \mu^T \frac{\partial \varphi}{\partial u^1} &= \lambda^T(\tau)\frac{\partial g}{\partial u^1} + \mu^T \frac{\partial \varphi}{\partial u^1} = 0 \\ \frac{\partial H}{\partial u^2} + \nu^T \frac{\partial \psi}{\partial u^2} &= \lambda^T(\tau)\frac{\partial g}{\partial u^2} + \nu^T \frac{\partial \psi}{\partial u^2} = 0 \end{aligned} \tag{5.9}$$

where row vectors

$$\frac{\partial H}{\partial u^i} = \left(\frac{\partial H}{\partial u_1^i}, \frac{\partial H}{\partial u_2^i}, \ldots, \frac{\partial H}{\partial u_{d_i}^i}\right)$$

and matrices

$$\frac{\partial \varphi}{\partial u^1} = \left[\frac{\partial \varphi_i\,(x,u^1)}{\partial u^1_j}\right] \qquad \begin{array}{l} i = 1,2,\ldots,k \\ j = 1,2,\ldots,d_1 \end{array}$$

$$\frac{\partial \psi}{\partial u^2} = \left[\frac{\partial \psi_i\,(x,u^2)}{\partial u^2_j}\right] \qquad \begin{array}{l} i = 1,2,\ldots,\ell \\ j = 1,2,\ldots,d_2 \end{array}$$

at $x = x^*(\tau)$, $u^i = p^{i*}(x^*(\tau))$.

If $x^*(\tau)$ is an interior point of X^*, then (5.7) and (5.8) imply that

$$\varphi_i\,(x,p^{1*}(x)) \quad , \quad i = 1,2,\ldots,k'$$

$$\psi_i\,(x,p^{2*}(x)) \quad , \quad i = 1,2,\ldots,\ell'$$

have stationary maxima at $x = x^*(\tau)$.
Hence

$$(5.10) \qquad \begin{array}{ll} \displaystyle\sum_{j=1}^{n} \frac{\partial \varphi_i}{\partial x_j} + \sum_{j=1}^{n}\sum_{r=1}^{d_1} \frac{\partial \varphi_i}{\partial u^1_r}\frac{\partial p^{1*}_r}{\partial x_j} = 0 & i = 1,2,\ldots,k' \\ \displaystyle\sum_{j=1}^{n} \frac{\partial \psi_i}{\partial x_j} + \sum_{j=1}^{n}\sum_{r=1}^{d_2} \frac{\partial \psi_i}{\partial u^2_r}\frac{\partial p^{2*}_r}{\partial x_j} = 0 & i = 1,2,\ldots,\ell' \end{array}$$

or, in vector form,

$$(5.11) \qquad \begin{array}{l} \mu^T \left[\dfrac{\partial \varphi}{\partial y} + \dfrac{\partial \varphi}{\partial u^1}\dfrac{dp^{1*}}{dy}\right] = 0 \\ \nu^T \left[\dfrac{\partial \psi}{\partial y} + \dfrac{\partial \psi}{\partial u^2}\dfrac{dp^{2*}}{dy}\right] = 0 \end{array}$$

where

$$\frac{\partial \varphi}{\partial y} = \begin{bmatrix} 0 & \dfrac{\partial \varphi_1}{\partial x_1} & \cdots & \dfrac{\partial \varphi_1}{\partial x_n} \\ \vdots & & & \vdots \\ 0 & \dfrac{\partial \varphi_k}{\partial x_1} & \cdots & \dfrac{\partial \varphi_k}{\partial x_n} \end{bmatrix}$$

$$\frac{\partial\psi}{\partial y} = \begin{bmatrix} 0 & \frac{\partial\psi_1}{\partial x_1} & \cdots & \frac{\partial\psi_1}{\partial x_n} \\ \vdots & & & \vdots \\ 0 & \frac{\partial\psi_\ell}{\partial x_1} & \cdots & \frac{\partial\psi_\ell}{\partial x_n} \end{bmatrix}$$

at $x = x^*(\tau)$, $u^i = p^{i*}(x^*(\tau))$.

By (5.9) and (5.11)

$$\lambda^T(\tau)\,\frac{\partial g}{\partial u^1}\frac{dp^{1*}}{dy} = \mu^T\,\frac{\partial\varphi}{\partial y}$$
$$\lambda^T(\tau)\,\frac{\partial g}{\partial u^2}\frac{dp^{2*}}{dy} = \nu^T\,\frac{\partial\psi}{\partial y} \tag{5.12}$$

or

$$\left(\frac{\partial g}{\partial u^1}\;\frac{dp^{1*}}{dy}\right)^T\lambda(\tau) = \left(\frac{\partial\varphi}{\partial y}\right)^T\mu$$
$$\left(\frac{\partial g}{\partial u^2}\;\frac{dp^{2*}}{dy}\right)^T\lambda(\tau) = \left(\frac{\partial\psi}{\partial y}\right)^T\nu \tag{5.13}$$

so that eqs. (5.6) can be written

$$\dot{\lambda}(\tau) = -\left(\frac{\partial g}{\partial y}\right)^T\lambda(\tau) - \left(\frac{\partial\varphi}{\partial y}\right)^T\mu - \left(\frac{\partial\psi}{\partial y}\right)^T\nu \tag{5.14}$$

for all τ such that $x^*(\tau)$ belongs to the interior of X^*. Thus, if constraints (5.7) are state-independent, (5.14) reduces to

$$\dot{\lambda}(\tau) = -\left(\frac{\partial g}{\partial y}\right)^T \lambda(\tau) \tag{5.15}$$

5.4 Sufficient Conditions for a Saddle-Point.

Here we shall give a sufficiency theorem that is the counterpart to Theorem 4.4; for a proof see Ref. 5.6. Other theorems can be found in Refs. 5.1, 5.3, 5.7 and 5.8.

Theorem 5.3. A strategy pair $\{p^{1*}(.), p^{2*}(.)\}$ that is playable for all $x^o \epsilon X$ is a saddle-point on X with respect to every strategy pair $\{p^1(.), p^2(.)\}$ that is playable at $x^o \epsilon X$ and whose terminating solutions $x(.) : [0, \tau_1] \to R^n$ are such that $x(\tau) \epsilon X$ for all $\tau \epsilon [0, \tau_1]$, if there exists a denumerable decomposition D of X and a continuous function $V(.) : X \to R^1$ that is continuously differentiable with respect to D such that

(i) $f_o(x, p^{1*}(x), u^2) + \text{grad } V_j(x) f(x, p^{1*}(x), u^2) \leq 0$ for all $x \epsilon X_j$, $u^2 \epsilon U^2(x)$, $j \epsilon J$, and

$$f_o(x, u^1, p^{2*}(x)) + \text{grad } V_j(x) f(x, u^1, p^{2*}(x)) \geq 0$$

for all $x \epsilon X_j$, $u^1 \epsilon U^1(x)$, $j \epsilon J$, where $\{ W_j, V_j) : j \epsilon J\}$ is a collection associated with V(.) and $D = \{X_j : j \epsilon J\}$, and

(ii) $V(x) = 0$ for all $x \epsilon \theta$.

5.5 Example: Collective Bargaining(*)

Whereas the collective bargaining example discussed in Sections 3.4 and 4.6 dealt with a process of negotiation during a strike, now we shall consider negotiations which allow for a strike but also for no strike. A second difference between the earlier problem and the present one lies in the fact that now we shall make no a priori assumptions concerning the dynamics of the process.

Let $[0, \tau_1]$ denote the unspecified interval during which negotiations take place. At $\tau \epsilon [0, \tau_1]$

$x(\tau)$ = offer by management of total wages per unit time

$y(\tau)$ = demand by labor for total wages per unit time

k = gross profit of company per unit time (**)

Let u(.), v(.), w(.) be bounded and measurable functions from $[0, \tau_1] \to R^1$ such that

$$u(\tau) \epsilon [0,1], \quad v(\tau) \epsilon [0,1], \quad w(\tau) \epsilon \{0,1\} \tag{5.16}$$

(*) Based on Ref. 5.9

(**) That is, profit rate before payment of wages.

The rates of change of offer and demand are controlled by management and labor, respectively. Thus,(*)

$$(5.17)\qquad \begin{aligned} \dot{x}(\tau) &= u(\tau) \\ \dot{y}(\tau) &= -v(\tau) \end{aligned}$$

with $x(0) = x^0$ and $y(0) = y^0$, the initial offer and demand, respectively.

Settlement is reached (termination) the first time offer equals demand, that is at time τ_1 such that

$$(5.18)\qquad y(\tau_1) - x(\tau_1) = 0$$

If $w(\tau) = 0$ implies no strike at time τ, and $w(\tau) = 1$ implies a strike at time τ, then

$w(\tau)[k - y(\tau)]$ = potential profit loss rate (due to management not acceding to labor's demand) during a strike

$w(\tau)\,x(\tau)$ = potential wage loss rate (due to labor not accepting management's offer) during a strike.

Now we propose the following motivations:

Management choose $u(\tau), \tau \in [0, \tau_1]$, so as to minimize the final offer $= x(\tau_1)$, and the potential profit loss during a strike

$$= \int_0^{\tau_1} w(\tau)[k - y(\tau)]\,d\tau ,$$

and to maximize.

the potential wage loss during a strike

$$= \int_0^{\tau_1} w(\tau)x(\tau)\,d\tau$$

Labor, on the other hand, choose $v(\tau)$ and $w(\tau)$, $\tau \in [0, \tau_1]$, so as to accomplish the converse.

The costs to management and labor, respectively, are then(**)

$$\int_0^{\tau_1} \{\alpha_1 u(\tau) + \alpha_2 w(\tau)[k - y(\tau)] - \alpha_3 w(\tau)x(\tau)\}d\tau$$

and

(*) Again, there is no need to introduce time, t, as a state component; this can be easily verified.

(**) Here we disregard constant terms which depend only on the given initial state.

and

$$\int_0^{\tau_1} \{\beta_1 u(\tau) + \beta_2 w(\tau)[k - y(\tau)] - \beta_3 w(\tau) x(\tau)\} d\tau$$

where the α_i and β_i , i = 1, 2, 3, are prescribed non-negative constants. If we assume equal weighting assigned to the three motivation terms, we are faced with a two-person zero-sum game.

It is convenient to use $x(\tau)$ and $z(\tau) = y(\tau) - x(\tau)$ as state variables, so that termination takes place when $z(\tau_1) = 0$. In terms of these variables, the cost is

$$\int_0^{\tau_1} \{u(\tau) + w(\tau)[k - z(\tau) - 2x(\tau)]\} d\tau \qquad (5.19)$$

Now consider strategies(*) $\mu(.)$ and $(\nu(.), \omega(.))$ where

$$u(\tau) = \mu(x(\tau), z(\tau))$$
$$v(\tau) = \nu(x(\tau), z(\tau))$$
$$w(\tau) = \omega(x(\tau), z(\tau))$$

Here, $\mu(.)$ is the strategy of the minimizing player, management, and $(\nu(,), \omega(.))$ is the strategy of the maximizing player, labor. We seek a saddle-point $\{\mu^*(,), (\nu^*(.), \omega^*(.))\}$ on

$$X = \{(x, z) \epsilon R^2 : 0 < x < k, z > 0\}$$

with target set

$$\theta = \{(x, z) \epsilon R^2 : 0 < x < k, z = 0\}$$

Upon use of the necessary conditions of Theorem 5.2 and of the sufficient conditions of Theorem 5.3(**), one can establish the following saddle--point (Ref. 5.9):

$$\left.\begin{aligned} \mu^*(x, z) &= 1 \\ \nu^*(x, z) &= 0 \\ \omega^*(x, \bar{z}) &= 1 \end{aligned}\right\} (x, \bar{z}) \epsilon X_1$$

(*) Again, it can be readily verified that time, t not be considered as an additional state variable.

(**) Since $X \cap \theta = \phi$, we use X^* in place of X in Theorem 5.3.

$$\left.\begin{aligned} \mu^*(x,\bar{z}) &= 1 \\ \nu^*(x,\bar{z}) &= 1 \\ \omega^*(x,\bar{z}) &= 1 \end{aligned}\right\} (x,\bar{z}) \in X_2$$

$$\left.\begin{aligned} \mu^*(x,\dot{z}) &= 1 \\ \nu^*(x,z) &= 1 \\ \omega^*(x,z) &= 1 \text{ or } 0 \end{aligned}\right\} (x,z) \in \bar{X}_2 \cap \bar{X}_3 \cap X$$

$$\left.\begin{aligned} \mu^*(x,\hat{z}) &= 0 \\ \nu^*(x,\bar{z}) &= 1 \\ \omega^*(x,\dot{z}) &= 0 \end{aligned}\right\} (x,z) \in X_3$$

where for $k \leqslant 2$

$$X_1 = \{(x,z) : 2x \leqslant k - 2z\} \cap X$$

$$X_2 = \{(x,z) : k - 2z < 2x < k - z\} \cap X$$

$$X_3 = \{(x,z) : k - z < 2x\} \cap X$$

and for $k > 2$

$$X_1 = \{(x,z) : 2x \leqslant 1 + k - 3z \text{ and } 2x \leqslant k - 2z\} \cap X$$

$$X_2 = \{(x,z) : k - 2z < 2x < k - z \text{ or } 1 + k - 3z < 2x < k - z\} \cap X$$

$$X_3 = \{(x,z) : k - z < 2x\} \cap X$$

In particular, the saddle-point strategy for labor calls for a strike whenever the offer falls below the potential profit, $x < k - y$.

References for Chapter 5.

[5.1] Isaacs, R., Differential Games, Wiley, N.Y., 1965.

[5.2] Blaquière, A. and Leitmann, G., Jeux Quantitatifs, Gauthier-Villars, Paris, 1969.

[5.3] Blaquière, A., Gérard, F., and Leitmann, G., Quantitative and Qualitative Games, Academic Press, N.Y., 1969.

[5.4] Friedman, A., Differential Games, Wiley, N.Y., 1971.

[5.5] Bryson, A.E., Jr., and Ho, Y.C., Applied Optimal Control, Blaisdell, N.Y., 1969.

[5.6] Stalford, H. and Leitmann, G., Sufficiency Conditions for Nash Equilibria in N-Person Differential Games, in Topics in Differential Games (ed. A. Blaquière), North-Holland, Amsterdam, 1973.

[5.7] Case, J.H., Toward a Theory of Many Player Differential Games, SIAM J. Control, Vol. 7, No. 2, 1969.

[5.8] Stalford, H. and Leitmann, G., Sufficient Conditions for Optimality in Two-Person Zero-Sum Differential Games with State and Strategy Constraints, J. Math. Anal. Appl., Vol. 33, No. 3, 1971.

[5.9] Leitmann, G., Collective Bargaining: A Differential Game, J. Optim. Theory Appl., Vol. 11, No. 4, 1973.

Appendix A: Integral and Terminal Costs

Let us consider a terminal cost $g_i(x(\tau_1))$ where $g_i(\cdot)$: $R^n \to R^1$ is of class C^1. We wish to deal with an equivalent cost in integral form.

We note that

$$g_i(x(\tau_1)) = g_i(x(0)) + \int_0^{\tau_1} \text{grad } g_i(x(\tau))f(x(\tau),u^1(\tau),\ldots,u^N(\tau))d\tau$$

However, since $x(0) = x^o$ is specified, so is $g_i(x(0))$. Thus, the integral cost differs from the terminal only by a constant. Thus, we need consider only the integral cost

$$\left.\begin{matrix} V_i(x^o,u(.)) \\ V_i(x^o,p(.),x(.)) \end{matrix}\right\} = \int_0^{\tau_1} \text{grad } g_i(x(\tau))f(x(\tau),u^1(\tau),\ldots,u^N(\tau))d\tau$$

which is of type (2.6).

Conversely, given an integral cost

$$\int_0^{\tau_1} f_o^i(x(\tau),u^1(\tau),\ldots,u^N(\tau))d\tau$$

we wish to deal with an equivalent cost in terminal form.

Let $x_{n+i}(\tau)$ be an additional state component such that

$$\dot{x}_{n+i}(\tau) = f_o^i(x(\tau),u^1(\tau),\ldots,u^N(\tau))$$

with

$$x_{n+i}(0) = 0$$

so that

$$x_{n+i}(\tau) = \int_0^{\tau_1} f_o^i(x(\tau),u^1(\tau),\ldots,u^N(\tau))d\tau$$

Thus, if we have integral costs for all $i \in \{1, 2, \ldots, N\}$ and we convert to terminal costs, we have an augmented state $\hat{x} = (x, x_{n+1}, \ldots, x_{n+N}) \in R^{n+N}$ and terminal cost functions $g_i(.)$: $R^{n+N} \rightarrow R^1$ where

$$g_i(\hat{x}(\tau_1)) = x_{n+i}(\tau_1)$$

Appendix B: Change of Interval

Consider a system with state equation

$$\frac{dx}{dt} = f(x,t,u) \in R^n \tag{B.1}$$

with $x(t_o) = x^\circ$, $t \in [t_o, t_1]$ with $t_1 > t_o$.

Suppose whish to convert to an equivalent system with independent variable $\tau \in [0,1]$. To do so introduce

$$x_{n+1} = t$$
$$x_{n+2} = t_1 - t_o$$
$$\tau = \frac{t}{x_{n+2}}$$

so that (B.1) becomes

$$\frac{dx}{d\tau} = x_{n+2} f(x, x_{n+1}, u) \tag{B.2}$$

with $x(0) = x^\circ$, $\tau \in [0,1]$, where

$$\frac{dx_{n+1}}{d\tau} = x_{n+2} \qquad \frac{dx_{n+2}}{d\tau} = 0 \tag{B.3}$$

with $x_{n+1}(0) = t_o$.

CONTENTS

Errata Corrige

Title: "Many player" instead of "Many players"

Page 62, following line 5, add:

and $\{ p^{1*}(\cdot), \ \hat{p}^2(\cdot)\}$ and $\{\hat{p}^1(\cdot), \ p^{2*}(\cdot)\}$ are playable x^o,

Title of paragraph 3: "Cooperative Differential Games" instead of "Cooperative Dipartimental Games"

Printed in the United States
By Bookmasters